To
Bo
Thi
For 'T' ser1Nt

AN ANGEL RODE
MY WING

By

Neil Levin

LEATHERNECK PUBLISHING
Oceanside, California

Published by   Leatherneck Publishing
A Division of Levin Publishing Group
http://www.leatherneckpublishing.com

Publisher: Lt Col H. Neil Levin, USMC (ret)

Edition: 10 9 8 7 6 5 4 3 2   SAN: 256-8799

Library of Congress Control Number: 2005938956

ISBN-13: 978-0-9771431-0-8
ISBN-10: 0-9771431-0-4 (previously 1-4208-0073-6)

Cover Photo: Lt Col David Althoff, USMC (ret)

Printed and Bound in Kansas City, MO
United States of America.
This Book is printed on Acid Free Paper

These stories of aerial combat have vigor and authenticity, which bring life to every page.
- *L a rry Wade, Author and Editor,*
The Coronado Journal

Neil and I flew many combat missions together in Vietnam and his portrayal of flying out of Chu Lai, South Vietnam are accurate and bring back many memories. A good read.
- *B ruce R. (Pete) Booher, Former VMA-224*
Marine Attack Pilot-Retired Delta Airline Captain

Neil Levin has used his well-honed reportorial skills to bring to light first hand, his experiences as a Marine attack aviator in Viet Nam. For those of us who lived those days with him, it conjures up memories of stifling heat, monsoon rains, lousy C rations and a uneven rolling aluminum runway that varied in length from day to day, but more significantly, the camaraderie of Marines in combat, doing what they do best.
- *Colonel Richard E. Hawes, USMC (Ret).*

Five of Neil Levin's stories included in this book were recently published in AERO Magazine, an international aviation magazine, in Hungary and well received in the Aviation Community.
- *Tamas' Szorad, Freelance journalist and*
columnist AERO Magazine

DEDICATION

Thomas E Mulvihill
COL. USMC
My Hero, my Mentor and my Friend
And
Alex Edgar Levin
My Hero, my Father and my Friend

ACKNOWLEDGEMENTS

I would like to acknowledge some special people who inspired and encouraged me to write my story. Without the encouragement from these people, I never would have written these stories and kept them inside.

My heartfelt thanks to:

My mother for always believing in me and always telling me "You can do this," no matter what "this" was.

My niece, Michelle, the first one to ask me to write what I kept bottled inside for years.

My sister, Jan and brother-in-law, Marvin for insisting I get started.

Carol and Jack Mendelson, friends and professional writers who convinced me I could and should write.

Larry Wade, a professional writer and editor, who encouraged me to write.

Friends and family who believe in me.

My loving wife, Laurie, who neither pushes or follows me, but stands by my side and encourages me to do what I believe I must.

Nancy King who helped me tremendously by editing the book. I respectfully refer to her as Drill Sgt. King because she is tougher than any Marine Drill Sgt. I ever met.

TABLE OF CONTENTS

PRELUDE

I never intended to write a book. A few significant events took place in my life that led me to want to share my beliefs, my philosophical thoughts and some of my more interesting flying experiences with my family, especially my children and grandchildren and with friends.

One of these events - my Grandmother, my Father's Mother passed on at the ripe old age of either 103 or 104. (No one is sure which age) My point is, she passed through my life and beyond and I loved her dearly yet when she died I realized there was very little I knew about that wonderful, talented, wise and loving woman. To this day, I learn more about her when I visit my Mother. Things like she waved signs pushing "Woman's Rights" on street corners long before it was fashionable or politically correct to do so. She was tiny, weighing less than one hundred pounds soaking wet, but I can imagine her standing there, head held high, looking people in the eye arguing about Woman's rights with fire in her eyes, but with a soft gentle smile on her face. Born and raised in Russia, she spoke in broken English with a foreign accent but with a direct yet quiet voice. She read a lot and educated herself. I learned she was a disciple of Margaret Sanger. She knocked door to door to spread the word about birth control. She even stood out in the snow on street corners, bundled up in warm clothing with a wrap around her head and cup in hand to collect money for a local hospital.

She was a Woman of peace. I yearn to learn more about her.

Although Grandma and I spent a lot of time together, especially watching John Wayne movies on Saturday afternoons when I was a little kid, I never knew any of these things from her.

It occurred to me I had thoughts, ideas and experiences to share with others and if I did, my grandchildren would have a better idea of who their grandfather is and my friends, who know most of my philosophies on life, could share some of my flying experiences. I wrote about my philosophies elsewhere. This book is more about my adventures in flying.

Another event - I visited the Vietnam War Memorial Wall in Washington, D.C. and I realized how lucky and fortunate I was not to be included among the names before me, many who were known to me. Others were friends. I didn't look them up, but just knew they were there.

As I sensed the emotion all around me and within me, I realized the people behind those names on that Wall all had stories to tell, but would never have the opportunity to tell them. I decided it was time to tell my story.

The book is about some of my Military and flying experiences while serving as a Naval

Aviation Cadet starting in 1953 to retirement as a Marine Lieutenant Colonel in 1973.

Some of the stories are humorous, some are not, but all are true. It encompasses two combat tours of duty in Vietnam. I realize any pilot putting on a pair of combat flight boots may have similar stories to tell.

I decided to share mine.

A CHANGE OF LIFE

The long train ride from the North Philadelphia station to Pensacola, Florida took a couple of days but that wasn't the hard part. The hard part was I left my life as a wise-ass-know-it-all kid from Jersey to God knows what. It was the April 4, 1953 and I just turned twenty-one years old a few days earlier. I was sworn into the United States Navy at the Naval Air Station at Willow Grove, PA a few weeks before as a Naval Aviation Cadet and headed south to Pensacola for flight training.

Known as Navcads, we held that rank until and if, we earned our Navy wings eighteen to twenty months later. We were then promoted to the officer ranks, either as an Ensign in the Navy or as a Second Lieutenant in the Marine Corps.

As the train rolled South, I thought of early that morning when I had breakfast with my Dad and my good buddy Syd, college roommate

1

and close friend, in a White Tower restaurant, the greasy spoons of the time, just outside of Camden, New Jersey.

Syd was a suave good-looking guy with long black hair, long before it was fashionable. He didn't have an ounce of fat on him and he looked like a combination of Rudolph Valentino and Tony Curtis. I remember how he used "Three Flowers Brilliantine" and "Pommade" to grease his hair and keep it in place. He had a terrific sense of humor, a gleam in his eye and a smile that made all the girls either want to have him, Mother him, or both. I always wondered how he did that, but looking back on it now I realize he always made a woman feel beautiful. He was a terrific dancer and one hell of a fun guy. He was so fast on his feet when he danced it seemed he could dance two directions at the same time. Actually later in life, he made dancing his career and owned a bunch of dance studios. I never forgot those early wild and crazy days with Syd and how much fun we had hanging out together. Of course, he always got the girl, but then that is another story.

My Dad and he were so proud of me and I acted like it was no big deal, when actually, I churned inside, not from fright, but leaving everybody and everything familiar to venture into an unknown area. I wasn't scared because my Dad taught me if something was done by anyone else, it could be done by me.

AN ANGEL RODE MY WING

As I boarded the train he waved goodbye, tears in his eyes, he reassuringly said, "You've got what it takes."

Armed with those words, it didn't occur to me then or later, I wouldn't earn my wings and become a Naval Aviator, even though I was briefed only 25 percent of Navcads complete flight training, I would succeed.

As we passed Baltimore and traveled south of the Mason-Dixon Line, I flashed back to when I was a little kid of twelve sitting on the banks of the Delaware River, which bordered my home town of Burlington, New Jersey, and how I watched the airliners flying overhead enroute from Philadelphia to New York and beyond. I fantasized about flying a plane, but of course, I never thought for a minute it was something I could actually do. My Dad took flying lessons at Burlington Air Park, a few miles out of town. He and his instructor took me up in a Piper Cub. My first flight and I was hooked.

The train rolled on and since I was never in the South before, I kept looking for plantations like Tara in "Gone With The Wind" with tall white towering columns typical of Southern architecture. We passed through a lot of farmland and many small towns. I never saw a plantation, but as I looked out of the train windows, I saw many dilapidated old buildings in towns and broken down barns on farms. I thought it must be what they meant by "the wrong side of the tracks" except it was the same on both sides. Of course, I'm just kidding.

3

Parts of the South were beautiful. I loved the tall trees with the moss hanging from them, rolling green hills and lots of colorful flowers. As people got on the train in the Southern towns, I could hear more and more Southern accents. I loved it. We had a gal in our High School that moved to Burlington from the deep South, I believe Mississippi. She was gorgeous with long flowing red hair and looked a lot more grown up than the girls I was used to in High School. I loved the way she asked me,"Are ya'll goin' to the big dance Saturday? If so I will save you a dance. My boyfriend is goin' to carry me there."

I always thought "to carry me there" was a strange thing to say, but it was what Southern girls said back then.

Back to the train, I started to realize I was a Yankee surrounded by Rebels and to many of them the Civil War was not over.

I wasn't alone on this trip. Of the six of us that took the qualifying physical and mental exams at Nas Willow Grove to become Navcads, only two of us qualified. A guy named Chuck and I. In typical fashion, the Navy had to have somebody in charge so they put Chuck in charge of me. That meant he carried our orders to check in at Pensacola and our meal vouchers. I never liked anybody to be in charge of me. I told him not to take the "in charge stuff" too seriously.

We finally arrived at downtown Pensacola. The town seemed strange to me. The only building that stood out was the San Carlos Hotel. I found out later Pensacola was a town steeped in history. After we took a taxi out to the Naval Air Station, we arrived at the Naval Schools Command and the pre-flight training headquarters for all the Navcads.

I stood in front of this large gray Navy building with huge columns in front and found the columns I was looking for in the South even if they weren't white. I joined others congregated and met a guy named George, which I will talk about later. We were all dressed in our civilian clothes waiting for induction into the Navy and issued Navcad uniforms. I wondered what the Hell am I doing here, but decided to go along with the program, whatever it is.

I considered myself special in New Jersey because I felt in control and most people made me feel like a pretty cool guy but this certainly was a different feeling. All of this would lead me into a completely new environment and a change of life.

PREFLIGHT

Earning my Wings was very important to me. I felt badly about not completing my College education and if I successfully completed the flight-training program while doing something I really wanted to do, was better than getting a college diploma and doing something I didn't.

As we stood outside of the building, a few drill sergeants showed up. They are all very trim and in real good shape. They seemed to shine, especially their shoes and belt buckles, and they wore these funny looking wide brimmed hats kind of tilted down so only their eyes showed.

I figured they must work out a lot. They asked us questions like where were we from and stuff like that.

"Welcome aboard," they said, an old Navy custom of welcoming people aboard ship. These drill sergeant guys seemed real nice and they made me feel good about being there.

AN ANGEL RODE MY WING

There were about forty of us. They had come from all over the country. Soon a Marine Captain came out of the building and told the Drill Sergeants to bring us inside.

"You are designated Pre-flight class 16-53," he said, "Because you are the class of the sixteenth week of 1953."

Each week a new class arrived and every Friday morning a Pre-flight class graduated. Kind of an assembly line for students, I thought.

As soon as we passed through those huge gray columns and entered the building our whole world changed. Those real nice Drill Sergeants turned into raving maniacs and started to scream and yell at us, stick their faces right into our faces and ask us stupid questions over and over again. They yelled so loud they can't hear us and made us answer all over again louder until we screamed back. They made us yell "Sir" at the beginning and end of each answer.

"Are you a low life brat who thinks this program will be like a walk in the park?" he shouted loud enough to break an eardrum.

"Sir. No sir," I yelled, and it got much worse.

This came as a complete shock to my system. Nobody, but nobody was allowed to yell at me like that without getting punched out. All the guys in my fraternity at College knew that and one of them is probably still bouncing down the stairs where I knocked him. My first inclination was to tell these jerks they could take this program and shove it, but fortunately, I realized in short order that was exactly what they wanted me to do.

They kept screaming DOR, which meant, "drop on request" or quit the Pre-flight program. If I quit or failed to graduate from the Navcad program, I would have to serve as an enlisted man in the Navy for a period of two years as stipulated in my contract. We immersed ourselves into the sixteen-week Pre-flight training program for the purpose of finding out if we had the right stuff to even enter the cockpit of an airplane. One of the purposes of pre-flight training was to weed out the meek and only pass the 25% who could take it. Flight training would come when and if we graduated. They figured if you passed, it was because you really wanted to be a Navy or Marine Corps pilot.

I decided they could throw whatever they had at me and I would take it and toss it right back to them because I was determined and smarter than they were.

I realize now we didn't have the advantage of seeing the movie "Officer and a Gentleman" which wasn't produced until many years later. If we had, we would have known what to expect because that movie was extremely accurate, except for it's location, about Navcads going through the Pre-flight program.

They hustled us around for hours, issuing us clothing, bedding and our bunk assignments. We were assigned four to a room. When lights out at 10:00 PM sharp and all was quiet, I could hear a guy sobbing in another room. He DOR'd in the morning.

I tried to sleep, but kept thinking about where I was and how I got here. I wish I could truthfully say something like I was very patriotic about the Korean War, while many of my friends at The Philadelphia College of Pharmacy and Science scrambled to get out of the Draft and I thought it was my duty to serve my Country. It sounds nice, but not true.

The truth is, while in my junior year at College, I realized Pharmacy was not for me. My Dad was a Pharmacist and I thought it was a good idea so I gave it a try. I never did take it too seriously though and I can't remember a grade above a "C." Due to most "Ds" and a couple "Fs," I had to pass by going to summer school at Temple University and another summer at the University of Pennsylvania. I studied Algebra at one and Zoology at the other.

It's a wonder I didn't get kicked out of school. I had a lot of fun, like when I made glucose suppositories in the lab, the assignment for the day. I thought I would have fun with the lab instructor. He looked over my work.

"Levin, why are you using tincture of lemon to make suppositories?" he asked.

"To make them taste better, of course."

I also recalled how I put on sneakers and black clothing and snuck into the school one dark night. I climbed in through the zoology lab window. I tried to steal the Algebra exam from the

Dean's office. I remember diving out of that same window as a security guard with a pistol chased me.

Yes, those were the days. I finally decided to leave school and realized I would be drafted. I also reasoned since I was going into the service; why not pick one instead. I liked boats so I went into the Navy Recruiting office in Philadelphia. The Navy recruiting officer said since I had well over sixty college credits, I could qualify to take officer training and maybe even pilot training.

So guess what I chose?

My mind turned off and I drifted off to sleep.

I breezed through pre-flight training because I had the right attitude and wanted it badly enough. Although the Drill Sergeants must not have thought I had the right attitude because of the constant conflict between them and me. I spent most Saturday mornings on the Parade Grounds, marching with a rifle on my shoulder as punishment for some of my indiscretions. I remember many of my friends waving at me as they headed to the main gate for liberty for the day. Liberty usually consisted of walking downtown Pensacola or going to the beach looking for girls.

We were allowed to have a maximum of fifty demerits without being washed out of the pre-flight program and I graduated with forty-five. Just to put them in proper perspective, getting caught outside smoking was five demerits and an hour of marching. We had a surprise inspection one day and since my closet was a complete mess, my buddies were afraid I would be washed out by failing the inspection and going over the maximum points. The inspecting officer was in the next room when I locked my closet and turned toward my roommates.

"I am going to the Infirmary to give blood for the Blood Bank," I said and left immediately, walked to the Infirmary and donated blood.

When I returned the inspection was over and the inspecting officer left the area. My buddies were still there studying. I confronted my pal George Kretschman.

"What did the inspecting officer have to say?" I asked. "Am I in serious trouble?"

"He said giving blood is very commendable." George replied. "He never asked why your locker wasn't open and ready for inspection."

I outsmarted them again.

Neil Levin

Mean Marine

The Commanding Officer of Pre-flight Training was a Marine Major Lufashynsky. We referred to him as the "mean Marine." Little could I have ever imagined at the time sixteen years later in 1969, I would be a Lieutenant Colonel and the Commanding Officer of the Pre-flight Training, which meant I was the "mean Marine."

FLIGHT TRAINING

Solo flight

It was a wonderful feeling after the Graduation Ceremonies on the Parade Grounds at NAS Pensacola. I breathed a sigh of relief because I came so close to being washed out.

Now it was onward and upward, literally, to flight training. Basic flight training was approximately a year and included training in the SNJ (pictured above). Now the games were over and it is time to get real and take all of this training seriously. My flying career was about to begin and although I had passed preflight training, I didn't know if I had what it takes to be a Navy or Marine pilot. Entering basic flight training meant solo flight, aerobatics, stalls and spins, instrument flight training, air to air gunnery, air combat fighter tactics, formation flight training, cross country navigational training, night flying, emergency training, and of course aircraft carrier landing qualification.

We flew out of various bases around Pensacola and Southern Alabama. As we progressed from one phase of training to another, we packed up our gear and checked in at the next base.

Each new base was pretty much like the one before. The check-in procedures were the same and so were the living conditions. The barracks were supposed to represent what living conditions were like aboard a Navy ship. Of course, our study habits and regulations were still in effect, but life got less restrictive as we progressed.

After completion of basic flight training, I went to Corpus Christi, Texas for advanced flight training. I flew the T-28 Trojan, F6-F Hellcat, the TV-2 Jet trainer and F9F-2 Panther Jet. The Trojan was for advanced instrument training, and the Hellcat was the first combat aircraft I flew. My jet indoctrination was in the TV-2 and the Panther Jet was for my jet fighter training.

Jet training was at NAS Kingsville Texas. This took six more months. When I accomplished all of that, I was awarded my gold Navy Wings and I was given a choice to be commissioned into the officer ranks as an Ensign in the Navy or as a 2nd Lieutenant in the Marine Corps. I chose the latter.

The flight training all started at NAS Whiting Field. We had 18 flights leading up to our solo flight and then we flew the A-19 Check flight. This was a thorough checkout of our flying abilities by a senior flight instructor other than our normally assigned flight instructor.

I remember my first milestone A-19 solo check flight well.

On a cool, clear, crispy day, I walked down to the flight line. All of my senses sizzled with the excitement of the moment. This day would determine whether I would continue my training or pack my duffle bag for good. There was a light breeze and I checked which runway was in use. I head for my A-19 check ride. I see five or six SNJs in the traffic pattern overhead on their downwind leg for landing. Some of them are returning after an hour and a half solo flight where they practiced all kinds of aerobatics out over Santa Rosa Island. If I succeed today, I will do that by myself tomorrow. This flight will be at least two hours long. I am just outside of Hanger 1 to meet my check pilot, Commander Brugger, for a pre-flight briefing. He is a tough one. If I pass my flight check from him, I must be ready.

I completed all the requirements of the check flight including three full stop landings. We stop and he climbed out.

"Just do what you have been doing and you will be all right," he said.

This is it, "My Moment of Truth." I line up my SNJ heading North into the wind at Pace field, a large grass field and push the throttle to full power. I'm airborne at sixty-five knots and feeling like a million bucks. I yell for joy and feeling I have this baby fully under control and nothing but nothing, will stop me from being a fighter pilot. This is the beginning.

I completed my third and final full-stop solo landing and taxied back to the area where my instructor was waiting.

He climbed into the back seat. "You did well. Take me home," he said.

I took off again with him in the rear cockpit and headed toward our home base.

The next day and I'm off on my A-20 flight. It's a great feeling to be up here by myself. I go out to Santa Rosa Island and wring this airplane out, meaning to fly the airplane to its maximum performance and to mine. I was a pretty good flight student because I managed to stay in the top ten percent of my class all the way through. Training was fairly standard except for a few interesting incidents.

FLIGHT LOG 23 APRIL 1954
CRASH LANDING

While flying formation flight training out of Saufley Field, I was taught how to fly in tight formation with other aircraft. Actually, we were taught how to perform all of the same maneuvers the Blue Angels perform at air shows.

I remember walking out to the flight line to strap myself into an SNJ, equivalent to the Air Force's AT-6, except the SNJ had a more powerful engine and the fuselage beefed up or strengthened for aircraft carrier landings. I love the smell of that plane. It smelled like banana oil. It probably had something to do with whatever substance they used to tighten the fabric to the aluminum frame.

I taxi on the taxiway toward the takeoff end of the runway. This is a formation flight, so I join up with the three other wingmen right after take-off. I line up in a four-plane echelon on the runway. I hear the words "cleared for take-off"

17

from Saufley tower and they shine a steady green light at me. My plane is number three for take-off and I start my roll as soon as number two is airborne.

Thumb ups – Ready to go.

There he goes and lifts off, so I follow … Full throttle to 36 inches of manifold pressure and whatever the propeller gives me between 2700 and 2900 rpm. Keep her lined up with the centerline and lift off at 65 knots. Throttle back to climb power settings with the engine and prop and pick up climb speed, about 90 knots, raise the wheels and flaps.

All is well and I see number two ahead of me starting his turn. I join on his wing by turning inside of him and match his speed. Since my radius of turn will be less than his, I can catch him even though I am at the same speed. This is standard procedure.

What a beautiful day to fly. I sure do love this stuff.

Suddenly, I get a severe vibration from the prop and the engine is running rough. Quick engine and fuel check. The fuel gauges on the console show all fuel tanks full and the fuel tank flow handles correctly placed. The fuel pressure gauge shows proper pressure. The problem might be the ignition harness and all I can do is to declare an emergency and try to nurse this bird back to Saufley Field, which is about a mile and a half behind me. I'm 250 feet over a heavily wooded area, the pines of Northern Florida.

There goes the engine!

The prop vibrated to a frozen position.

I look at it and it looks back at me. It isn't even wind milling. I have no choice but to crash land this thing. Well, now I know this is what training is all about. I practiced this enough, so let's do it for real. I can do this. Keep your cool. Pick up a 90-knot glide speed and maintain it. Call May Day to the tower, then my position.

I may luck out.

There is a small farm off of my right wing. It will be close, but I prefer to crash on that farm instead of those trees.

Turning, I stretch my glide to make it. If I drop my wheels, I will never make the field due to the increased drag. My only chance is to maintain glide speed and drop right down to the treetops and fully extend the wing flaps which will trade speed for increased lift and pop over the trees and down into the field, wheels up.

Normally, I would think about all those farmer's daughter jokes, except that I am kind of busy right now.

Oh My God, there are cows all over this field. I didn't think about that. Wow, I never saw cows run so fast. They are getting out of my way. They act like they have been through this sort of thing before. I'm glad somebody has. It sure is my first time. I clear the trees, wheels up, brace for crash landing and open the canopy. All ignition switches off and the fuel cut-off switch activated. Get as slow as I can before letting her hit.

The ground is coming up fast now. I hope I don't burn.

I hit and it jars the hell out of me as I plow up the field. The aircraft stopped. Except for tearing up the under belly of this plane, digging up crops and scaring the hell out of myself, I am okay! Whew, I made it.

I scramble out of the plane in case she catches fire. Here comes the farmer. He sure is walking casually.

"Hey, I called Saufley tower as soon as you hit," he said. "They'll pick you up in a chopper and send a crane to carry the airplane back."

"Has this ever happened in your field before?" I asked.

He smiled. "I have a standing agreement for a cash settlement every time one of you scares my cows."

I thought, those cows knew what they were doing.

FLIGHT LOG 19 NOV. 1954
JET AEROBATICS

F9F-2 Panther Jet

On this date, I flew an F9F-2 Panther jet and still a cadet in advanced flight training. Since the Panther only had one seat, the instructor chased me in another aircraft. This was an introduction to jet aerobatics. We did all the simple stuff, when he told me to do a loop.

Okay, a loop is pretty basic in this aircraft. Here we go, I dive down to 5000 feet to pick up 350 knots. Now full power and pull the nose up with the stick back to 4 g's. Sure is hazy today and I won't have much of a horizon to judge my nose position. How come the airspeed is down to 180 knots already? Oh crap, I misread my airspeed indicator. I started this loop at 250 knots instead of 350 knots. I will never have enough airspeed to get over the top of the loop.

Sure enough, the instructor is on my tail and yelling at me over the radio.

"Abort the loop, you're too slow," he bellows.

"Wilco," I answered.

Abort the loop

I must have my nose up to about a 45 degree position above the horizon, so if I roll inverted, I can drop the nose back to level flight and then roll back to right side up and start all over again. This should be a piece of cake.

Okay, a gentle roll, what's this? The nose isn't falling and I'm not inverted. Damn haze. I can't figure out what my airplane is doing.

Quick check of my instruments. I'm not 45 degrees nose up, but straight up so when I tried to roll, I spiraled straight up.

The airspeed is now at zero and I enter a hammerhead stall. The aircraft starts backing down like falling backwards. The aircraft tumbled head over heels, not flying but falling. How the hell do I recover from this maneuver? Full power and let go of the controls. I figure this airplane can fly better than me, so let it do its thing to start flying again.

The aircraft is in an inverted spin. Full back stick and idle on the throttle.

It worked and I return in a normal, upright spin, something I recognize I can recover from.

Opposite rudder from the rotation of the spin and full forward stick. There, the spin stopped, so I neutralize the controls and I come into a normal dive. Now, I pull out of the dive and return to straight and level flight.

I breathe easy again.

The instructor remained awfully quiet during all of this. He was right on my tail so when I started to back down, he had to get out of my way.

"I don't know whether to ground you or recommend you for the Blue Angels," he said. "I never saw an aircraft do what you just made that one do. Now quit fooling around and do it right."

I did.

The rest of my flight training was pretty routine.

A few weeks later, I earned my Navy Wings and became a Marine Pilot.

2nd Lieutenant

MEANWHILE, ON THE GROUND

I found I really loved to fly and actually felt more comfortable in the air than on the ground. I felt so at peace with myself, confident and completely in control while flying an airplane. I must admit there were times when I wasn't completely in control as in the preceding chapter, but for the most part I did less stupid things in the air than on the ground.

On the ground I looked for the angle to get around some regulation or find a way to beat the system. While in the air, I focused on what I was doing and military and aviation regulations were my law.

I was kind of a maverick in my twenties and seldom did what was expected of me, but more than not, I did whatever I wanted. For example, I got married while in advanced flight training still a Navcad in Kingsville, Texas, against all regulations.

AN ANGEL RODE MY WING

I met Mary Alice Bunch, a pretty Southern Belle from Mobile, Alabama. We dated frequently during the last few months of my basic flight training while I was stationed at NAS Barin Field in Foley, Alabama. A portrait artist, she lived with her art studio in her parent's home. Her brother, Alonzo attended Auburn University and was seldom home on weekends so I spent many weekends staying in his room when my flight schedule permitted.

We weren't paid very much even by '50's standards. Navcads were paid $108.00 per month. We didn't receive flight pay, which always amazed me, since the flight students, college graduates and already commissioned as officers, did get flight pay. Officially designated "hazardous duty pay" we Navcads flew the same hazards as the officer flight students. They were also allowed to marry, but we were not.

I bummed a ride with some buddies on a long 4th of July weekend and drove 825 miles to Mobile, Alabama. We married in Gulfport, Mississippi, spent one night in Biloxi, Mississippi, and I drove back to Texas all in the same weekend. That alone could have washed me out of the Navcad program and change my entire future. My new wife arrived by Greyhound bus three months later. I met her at the bus station and we set up house in a one-room efficiency apartment in a quiet neighborhood in the middle of Corpus Christi, Texas. The kind of apartment with a tiny kitchen and a bed hidden upright in the wall that folded down.

I was stationed forty-five miles away, but I figured I could keep my marriage a secret better if she didn't live close to my base.

We rented the apartment for $62.50 a month. That didn't leave us much to live on. My wife planned to show up with $350.00 and get a job, but instead she arrived with $35.00 and got pregnant. Poor thing, she got so sick she couldn't work and I could only see her on weekends and sometimes for a few hours in the evening. I had to be back in the cadet barracks at Kingsville for lights out at 10:00 PM each evening. I flew night training missions quite often during the week, so it wasn't uncommon for us not to see each other for a week at a time.

Mary Alice couldn't cook, except for steak and we certainly couldn't afford to eat steak often, so she surprised me once with okra. I made her promise me she would never make it again. In fact, if I ever have to give up something for lent, it will be okra.

Somehow, we made it through the remainder of my flight training. We appreciated what hardship could be when we looked in the refrigerator and cupboard and found them empty. Once we were having breakfast, which consisted only of cocoa, on a Saturday morning when the mail came and Mary Alice got a $400.00 check from her Aunt. Mary Alice painted a portrait of her Uncle and refused to take a commission for it.

Her Aunt, hearing of our financial hardship, sent it anyhow.

My aunt and uncle also helped and my mother and father helped us quite a bit. Other members of both of our families, who wanted to give us wedding gifts, sent us money instead because at the time that was what we really needed.

I have been asked, why I got married when I knew it would be difficult. It was because I had lost friends in aircraft training accidents and thought there was a good chance I might not live through training. I wanted to experience marriage and fatherhood while I could.

We divorced eighteen years later and I re-married since. It is not easy to be married to a Military pilot. Our marriage had its ups and downs like many marriages, but I must say in all due respect to my first wife, I appreciate those early years and all the hardships we withstood together, not to mention she gave me four great kids.

FLYING WITH THE BIG BOYS

AD Skyraider

In early January 1955, I drove through the main gate of MCAS Cherry Point, NC for the first time as a brand new 2nd Lieutenant proudly wearing my gold bars and wings. I was now a Marine Jet Fighter Pilot on my way to join my first Marine

Squadron. Those wings of gold were Navy wings and all Marine Pilots are Naval Aviators, having gone through Naval Aviation Training. In fact even though the Marine Corps is not a part of the Navy, it is part of the Navy Department and answers to the Secretary of the Navy under the Secretary of Defense and Marine Corps Aviation is funded by the Navy.

As I drove around the base trying to find the 2nd Marine Aircraft Wing Headquarters, I noticed the base was planned like a small city, self-contained with everything you could possibly need to sustain comfortable living for a family without going outside of the base for months. All Marine bases are like that except in many cases you could leave out the comfortable part.

I finally found the Wing Headquarters Building and reported to the administration officer and sent in to see the Colonel, the officer in charge of administration. He welcomed me into the Marine Corps and I felt like a Marine for the first time.

My excitement got shot in the foot, however, when I was told the jet squadron I was to join was being sent overseas to Korea in just a few weeks. I had my heart set on joining a Marine Jet Fighter Squadron, but the Korean War was over and I had my first child due in four months. I opted for assignment to VMC-2, a Marine Composite Squadron, so I could stay at Cherry Point for a while. VMC-2 was a prop squadron flying the AD Skyraider, a powerful airplane with a four bladed prop. The Squadron specialized in reconnaissance and air intelligence. The plane carried a lot of radar equipment and also capable of carrying a huge load of bombs, rockets and napalm.

After reporting to VMC-2, I learned the Squadron had not had a new pilot join them for at least a year. These were seasoned veteran pilots and I was the new guy on the block. I must admit when I first joined the squadron, I thought I was a pretty good hotshot pilot. I had excellent grades in my advanced flight training leading up to my Wings.

After spending a year and a half flying with these guys, I admit I really learned to fly the Marine way. Although tough for a while and hard to keep up with them, they took no excuses and demanded perfection. They flew hard, played hard and drank hard. I learned all of that stuff.

I walked into the ready room one foggy morning with the cloud cover at the instrument minimums for the base. The ceiling was 200 feet and visibility one-quarter mile. I figured we would spend the morning having ground instruction or playing acey-ducey in the ready room, standard procedure while waiting to fly. Much to my surprise, the operations officer came into the ready room with a new flight schedule.

"Launch 'em. We're an all weather squadron, so go get some practice," he said.

I took off alone in an AD4N and was in the soup right after take-off. I climbed to 9,500 feet en-route to Norfolk, the first leg of what we call a short round-robin flight. I passed over Norfolk, VA and headed for Raleigh, NC. Norfolk center changed my altitude a couple of times, but for the most part it was a routine instrument flight. Still in the soup I ended back over Cherry Point at 9000 feet. I entered the top of a stack of planes from 1500 feet to 9000 feet with an aircraft in the holding pattern every 500 feet. As one aircraft made its approach to the landing pattern, they lowered our holding altitude 500 feet. After quite a while, I was cleared to make my approach turn to the airfield where I was picked up by ground-controlled approach radar, known as GCI and given headings and altitude information constantly during my approach.

A GCA (Ground Control Approach) operator picked me up at 1200 feet and five miles out. He could see my aircraft's image on his radar screen and he talked to me on the radio "Turn left ten degrees, steady, turn right five degrees," and so on. "You are twenty feet above glide slope, increase your rate of descent. You are on glide slope and on heading. Looking good, hold what you have."

I practiced this many times in my training, so it was a piece of cake except normally I would break out of the clouds about 750 to 800 feet. I was still in the soup and passing 500 feet. I started to get a little nervous and was ready to break it off soon and go to my alternate airfield, which was Norfolk, when I realized the weather remained at minimums and meant I wouldn't break out until 200 feet.

I was at 300 feet, 250 feet and still couldn't see anything. At 200 feet I was ready to add full power and climb when I saw the runway lights just ahead and below me. I plunked that airplane on the runway and as I rolled out, I thought, sure glad that was supposed to be practice, otherwise it would have scared the hell of me.

I got a lot of experience for a rookie pilot the first few months, like an engine failure right after take off. I switched the fuel valve to a different fuel tank and quickly started it again. The engine failure occurred because I took-off on a near empty tank not re-fueled by the ground crew at Anacostia Naval Air Station in Washington, DC. It was my fault for not checking the tank visually during pre-flight inspection.

There was a night flight one hundred miles off of Cape Hatterras out over the Atlantic Ocean where we intercepted another airplane with our radar. I had an excellent radar observer in the rear compartment who located the airplane and gave me headings to fly to intercept him. It's a good thing he was in the plane with me because I learned about night vision fixation and vertigo all at once when he informed me that we were in a tight spiral and rapidly losing altitude.

He yelled, "Get on your instruments and level your wings. Now pull up. You are flying us into the water."

He was right.

AN ANGEL RODE MY WING

The incident was very similar to the tragedy when John Kennedy, jr. crashed into the ocean off of Long Island.

When you are a rookie, the trick is to get enough experience before you kill yourself. I got the experience, didn't kill myself and after a year and a half in that first squadron I felt real good about my flying.

I had been flying the AD4N and AD5N when we got a new type of airplane, the AD5W and it had a big radar pod under the fuselage. We called it "the guppie." It had some weird flight characteristics, like a whipstall to the right if you got too slow on landing and if you got into a spin, the procedure was to bail out. They were still doing spin tests on the AD5W at the Patuxent River, MD flight test center.

I strolled into the ready room one morning and was informed I was taking an AD5W to Lakehurst, New Jersey for radar modifications and was to pick up another AD5W and fly it back to Cherry Point. I informed the operations officer that I wasn't checked out in the AD5W yet. His comment was " Okay, check yourself out in the airplane on the way to Lakehurst."

I was finally considered to be one of the "big boys."

FLIGHT INSTRUCTOR
AIR-TO-AIR GUNNERY

The Marine Corps decided to merge the three Composite Squadrons with the three Photo Squadrons, one in each Aircraft Wing, and VMC-2 became VMCJ-2, a Photo Reconnaissance Squadron. The good news, we inherited the Photo Squadron's F9F6-P swept-wing jet aircraft. The bad news, the other Squadron's Commanding Officer was senior to ours and our Skipper was assigned to another duty station.

The first order of duty was to check each other out in each other's aircraft. We started training the jet pilots out in the ADs. I noticed getting us checked out in the jets was put on the back burner and none of us were trained. I also noticed one of our pilots suddenly transferred to a Transport Squadron, then another a week later.

I saw the writing on the wall and made a decision to request a transfer to the Naval Air Training Command in Pensacola as soon as possible. I would become a flight instructor there, at least flying tactical type aircraft instead of multi-engine C119 Flying Boxcars. I heard once you transferred into transports, you never returned to either fighter or attack squadrons. You seemed to disappear like a sock you put into the washer that never came out.

My transfer came through within 10 days. I figured I helped the Marine Corps solve their problem of re-locating pilots. I was lucky and ordered to report to Pensacola for training as an Air-to-Air Gunnery flight instructor. Air-to-air gunnery means firing live ammunition from an aircraft at an airborne target such as a cloth sleeve or banner. Air-to-ground gunnery is firing at targets on the ground from an aircraft. I would fly out of Barin Field located in Foley, Alabama.

Meanwhile promoted, I reported to Pensacola as a 1st Lieutenant.

Congratulations says Dad

I spent March and April of 1956 undergoing intensive flight training. I quickly discovered being a flight instructor wasn't as easy as I thought. Before you instructed any students, you had to become one yourself all over again and much harder than just flying an aircraft according to a set curriculum and a completely different concept of flying. As an instructor, you had to make the airplane do exactly as you described it was doing to a student.

For example, "All right now, we roll in 45 degrees of bank to the left and pull the nose up 45 degrees above the horizon and maintain that position until we have turned 90 degrees. There it is, now we drop the nose 45 degrees below the horizon and continue turning at the same rate until we have completed a 180 degree turn and we are back to our starting altitude and have rolled out of our turn on a heading of 360 degrees."

Sounds simple enough and it is, but doing it and talking about it at the same time is a learned process. It gets even more exciting when you are teaching air-to-air gunnery.

I instructed out of Barin Field and taught air-to-air gunnery in both the SNJ and later in the T-28. I also had the job of flight instructor to flight instructors in training. I also taught instrument flying in the T28 and the twin engine SNB Beechcraft to students.

Once the students flew the gunnery pattern with instructors satisfactorily, they were assigned a single instructor and the instructor towed either a sleeve or a banner type target for them to fire at. They fired a single 30-caliber machine gun in the SNJs mounted in the front part of the cockpit and synchronized to fire through the propeller. One of the problems was, if the student wasn't careful and accelerated his engine in his dive toward the target too fast he could create an over speed condition with his propeller and actually fire a hole in it. When this happened, and it did occasionally, it caused a vibrating propeller and rough running engine. The students flying the T28 fired two 50-caliber machine guns, wing mounted in gun pods hung below each wing.

There were six students assigned to a gunnery flight. Once they rocked in to their dives on the target, I would be busy flying the tow plane and keeping my eye on all six of them at different stages of their air-to-air gunnery runs, talking to them all and writing down chicken scratches, only I could decipher, on my knee pad strapped to my thigh above the knee. I used those writings later during the debriefing of the flight. It was important I made observations on every run by each student. They normally made about ten runs each so I deciphered a lot of chicken scratches.

I learned a lot about using airspace so they could make as many runs as possible. I gave them headings to fly in echelon formation, lined up side by side, at the end of the outbound leg and steer them to the cross leg of the target area. Meanwhile I made maneuvers with my plane so as soon as they rolled out on their new heading, I had the tow plane and the target in position for them to fire. The gunnery target area was over the Gulf of Mexico, south of Pensacola. We flew out 20 miles and parallel the coast for 60 miles and back in 20 miles and then return to Barin Field.

I didn't realize it then but all of this mastering of airspace would come in handy later in combat in Viet Nam when I was coming off of a target and needed to rendezvous my flight. I was able to easily give each of them a heading and an altitude to fly so we all ended up in the same airspace in combat formation.

Things usually went normally except for a few engine mishaps. One of my students had an engine failure and we were too far from the coast to make it to dry land so I sent my other students home, called "May Day," dropped my tow target and got on his wing. I managed to talk him down properly to make a crash landing in the Gulf.

He hit the water and skipped a couple of times like when you throw a flat rock into a lake. The plane dipped nose down momentarily and then shortly resurfaced. He climbed out of the cockpit and signaled with thumbs up he was okay. It floated for a while then sank. By that time, he inflated his Mae West and the raft, which is neatly folded under the seat of his parachute. He did it by the book and was just fine. Not a scratch on him. I circled over him until the Coast Guard helicopter arrived and picked him up and flew home.

One time, I had a rough running engine in a T28 about 10 miles south of NAS Pensacola, so I headed there to make a precautionary landing. About 5 miles out my engine quit so I made a dead stick emergency landing on their main runway.

We instructors, most Navy officers, were a pretty close bunch. A couple of us were Marines, but we held our own through the normal ready room jokes and pranks. We flew a lot, sometimes flying three flights during the day and chased the students on a night round-robin flight, flying over a predetermined course and landing at the starting point.

In all that time, my aircraft only got hit by one bullet in the tail.

After three years as a flight instructor, I was due for transfer, and hoped a transfer to that elusive jet fighter squadron, but instead I was ordered to training in California as a Forward Air Controller and Air Liaison Officer with the Ground Marines.

Forward Air Controller Class
Neil - Center Front

After training in Coronado, CA. for two months, I went to Okinawa for overseas duty and very unhappy about the transfer because flying was not the priority and I would be separated from my family for twenty-two months. I didn't know it at the time, but that training would later save my life in combat in Viet Nam.

PERILS OF PAULINE

J-3 Piper Cub

    I lived in Foley, Alabama while stationed at Barin Field. My next-door neighbor, a retired Air Force Officer, worked as a crop-duster pilot flying out of a small private airport five miles north of Foley in Summerdale with only a barn for a hanger and a grass strip runway two thousand feet long about one hundred feet wide fenced at both ends and sides. Three aircraft were kept in the hanger, a J3 Piper Cub, very light with wide balloon tires, a Piper Cub Cruiser, a little larger and heavier and a Stearman Bi-plane. All had two main landing gear or wheels and a tail wheel. The Cubs had flaps for higher lift capacity at slower speeds and all three had two seats, one front and one back. Spray or dust tanks containing insecticide were attached under the wings when crop-dusting.

I flew with my neighbor on a spraying mission and fell in love with crop dusting immediately. He showed me all the ropes and let me try it. I loved to fly with my wheels just above the crops and climb straight up just before reaching the tall pine trees or hedgerows, bordering each field.

I flew with him a couple times and got pretty good at it. The airport owner asked me to work for him crop-dusting. I explained I was a career Marine pilot and couldn't work outside of the Marine Corps on a professional basis without permission from the Corps. I could not accept pay for flying. He suggested I fly for him and since he closed the airport on Sundays, I could fly any of the three airplanes for personal use each Sunday and he would provide the gas as pay.

Life was so simple back in those days. I took the deal.

I flew crop-dusting early in the morning, just after sunrise, then worked at Barin Field flying two or three air-to-air gunnery flights during the day and once in a while got in another crop-dusting flight at dusk.

AN ANGEL RODE MY WING

Once a month I took a field representative from the Southern Bell Telephone Company up and we flew along forty miles of telephone poles from Gulf Shores to and along the causeway entering Mobile, Alabama. We flew at top-of-pole level so he could inspect each one for damage. We usually flew the J-3 Cub because it would fly as slow as thirty-five miles per hour, giving him a better view.

I enjoyed the work because I love to fly and I also had free access to the planes and the airport on Sundays.

While other young couples took Sunday drives around Baldwin County, Alabama looking for azaleas, my first wife Mary Alice and I soared above about seven thousand feet taking in the sights and having fun.

"Look at the beautiful colors and see how the farmer's fields are lined up with north-south and east-west boundaries," I said.

"It's so beautiful. Where are we goin?" she asked in her deep South Alabama accent.

"I would like to practice some emergency landing approaches."

"Well now, just how do you do that?"

"It's best if I have no idea when the emergency will occur so I will fly around for a while and you say "cut" at any time you're ready."

"What all happens then?"

"I will cut the engine, pick out a field and glide down and approach it for landing. Just before

45

landing, I will re-start the engine and climb back up to altitude."

"You know, Kneeyall, I don't think I like it. What if the engine doesn't re-start?"

"Then we will land in the field."

"Now Neil, why do you want to do such a crazy thing as cut off a perfectly good engine? You're always wantin' to do stuff like that. Can't we just go flyin' around like other people?"

"Because it will give me practice making dead stick landings while we have a good engine. If we have an engine quit unexpectedly someday, wouldn't you feel better knowing I can land us safely?"

"Well, since you put it that way, I guess so."

"Okay, cut," she said meekly.

"There, the engine is shut down. Notice how quiet it is? We are now in a glider. I am heading for that nice green field about two miles off our right wing."

"Aren't they power lines just short of that field?"

"Yes, but it's the best field around and we can approach into the wind and clear those power lines easily."

"Okay, we are now one thousand five hundred feet over the field and we circle for our landing approach."

I clear the power lines and drop down into the field. Now restart the engine. There it goes, full throttle and climb back up.

"See, no sweat. You sure are quiet back there."

"Yeah, I'm quiet. I'm scared to death. Let's not do that anymore."

"Okay."

I flew often on Sunday afternoons, sometimes taking Mary Alice and occasionally taking friends from my Squadron at Barin Field and their families for rides around Foley and over Mobile Bay or Gulf Shores.

One Sunday, I asked Mary Alice to pack a picnic lunch and wear a bathing suit.

"Where are we goin'?" she asked.

"The beach at Gulf Shores." I replied.

"Where will we land?"

"On the beach."

"Now, how are we goin' to land there with all the people in the way?"

"We'll land on a secluded part of the beach near the western end of the island. We have balloon tires on the plane and I will land on the hard sand near the surf, have lunch and go swimming"

We approach the beach and no one's in sight. Strong left crosswind but nothing we can't handle. Get this baby as slow as I can and ease her onto the sand and let the tail wheel down. It will grab the sand and slow us down quickly.

"There, we are down. Let's eat."

After a nice lunch and fun frolicking in the warm waves of the Gulf, we loaded our stuff into the plane and started our takeoff roll.

"Uh oh, trouble," I said.

"What!" she replied nervously.

"I didn't see that log ahead of us. I'm going to try to jump over it."

Full back stick rapidly and we hopped right over it and back on the sand to finish our takeoff roll.

"Sorry if I scared you. It was no big deal."

On another Sunday venture, I told her we were going to fly over Mobile Bay, have lunch and go swimming again.

She assumed we would land on the beach like a few other times.

"Should I pack a lunch? "she asked.

"No, we will get a hamburger and a coke at a bait shop near Fort Morgan."

Fort Morgan is a historical fort built in 1834 and used during the Civil War to guard the entrance to Mobile Bay, protect the Southern Fleet and keep the Southern supply lines open to the port city of Mobile, Alabama. The fort was captured on August 23, 1864 by Admiral David Farragut of the Northern Fleet during the famous Battle of Mobile Bay. He then proceeded through the entrance to the Bay with his eighteen ships and destroyed the Southern Fleet.

The Bay was heavily mined (called torpedoes in those days). When a fleet spotter sighted mines, and the lead ship, the iron bottomed ship Tecumseh sank, Admiral Farragut commanded his flag ship to take the lead and spoke his famous quote, "Damn the torpedoes! Go ahead, full speed."

AN ANGEL RODE MY WING

We flew over the bay and circled Fort Morgan. I previously practiced short field takeoffs and landings with the plane on the Summerdale landing strip so I had full confidence I could land and takeoff inside the Fort on a large courtyard the size of a small field.

"We're going to land inside the fort," I said.

"Now I know you all are nuts. You're kidding, right? Please tell me you're kidding."

"We can land there. I practiced this. Trust me, it will be all right."

We approach the wall, low and slow with full flaps and lots of engine power. Over the wall, dump the nose down and power off to idle followed by full back stick slamming the tail-wheel down on the field and get on the brakes hard. That is the same technique we used landing tail-wheel planes aboard aircraft carriers, except there we had a tail-hook and cable to stop us.

We taxied over to a corner of the courtyard and parked the plane, walked a block to a bait and tackle shop with a small restaurant and got our hamburgers.

After lunch, we returned to Fort Morgan and I pushed the plane back against the wall to provide more takeoff space.

Neil Levin

Fort Morgan - Landed in courtyard

This would be close, but I knew I could make it. I started the engine, ran it to full power locking the brakes then released the brakes starting our takeoff roll toward the opposite wall. Mary Alice didn't have anything to say. Lord only knows what she was thinking as I headed toward that wall. As soon as I had minimum takeoff speed I lifted the plane right over the wall with a few feet to spare.

"Now for the fun part. Let's go swimming."

"Where, on the beach?"

"No, on a sand bar."

"What sand bar?"

"There's a sand bar five miles out in the Gulf. You can only see it at low tide when it is exposed and it's low tide now."

"Here we are, landing on the bar."

"Let's get a quick swim in before the incoming tide covers the bar."

We went in the water for a while close by the plane.

"Isn't this a great adventure?"

"Yes, but don't you think we should get out of here? The tide is coming in pretty fast."

"I guess you're right. We only have about five minutes left before the bar disappears."

"Wow, we took off with water on our wheels. I played it a little close. Look at all the sharks down there. I didn't notice them before."

"Believe me, I've been watchin' them."

Looking back on it now, I realize Mary Alice had tremendous confidence in my ability to fly. I took chances, but they were actually calculated, acceptable risks. I practiced everything before I involved her in any risks, including landing on the beach and the sand bar. I took calculated risks crop-dusting every day in the same plane. Of course, the plane's owner had no idea about my Sunday afternoon adventures, only how much gas I used.

Mary Alice was a good sport going along with my young foolish antics or maybe she just wanted to get out of the house.

I am sure there were times when she felt like the star of the old movie " Perils of Pauline" where Pauline got into ridiculous dangerous predicaments and was rescued at the last minute.

THE GROUND MARINES

I arrived in Okinawa in the summer of 1958 and assigned to the 3rd Battalion, 3rd Marine Regiment, 3rd Marine Division as the Battalion Air Liaison Officer and Forward Air Controller. Recently promoted to the rank of Captain, I relieved a Captain and a Lieutenant who held those positions. The Battalion was known as the 333 and it had about one thousand Marine personnel in it.

The Battalion was based at Camp Bishagawa, formerly an abandoned and condemned Army base. In typical fashion, if it's cheap and available, the other armed services gave it to the Marines to fix up and use. We proudly accepted the task.

The officers I relieved were so glad to see me they insisted I let them show me the small local town a few miles from the base. That was my first mistake.

AN ANGEL RODE MY WING

I woke up as the sun's rays hit my face in the morning with the worst hangover I can ever remember. I was flat on my back in a ditch just outside of a small hut.

Soon an Okinawan woman came out of the hut and said, "Good morning, Neil San."

I have no idea how she knew my name, but after taking a good look at her, I was glad I woke up in the ditch.

I had to get used to a few things like the smell of the island. Space was a factor on Okinawa so when flat land wasn't available for farming, they terraced the hills. They used every available inch of farmland and fertilized it with human and animal waste. The whole island smelled like someone just went to the bathroom. I never got used to that smell. Another thing I had to adapt to, was a completely different environment with the Ground Marines. Although the same rank as most other officers in the Battalion, I had to earn their respect. I was singled out as an aviator instead of as a Marine Officer and I had to prove to them I was as smart, as proud and as tough.

They referred to me as the "Zoomie" because I came from the Marine Air Wing and a minority of one. I was used to being a minority as a Jewish kid growing up in an Italian and Polish small town in New Jersey. I knew how to gain their respect, by being myself, knowing my job as well as they knew theirs. It didn't take long. Things like leading the Battalion at the end of a fifteen-mile forced march with full packs on our backs in ninety-degree heat. Many of the men dropped like flies along the roadside from heat exhaustion. I gained a healthy respect for Navy Corpsmen who carried heavy equipment, ran back and forth enduring the same heat, to treat fallen Marines.

They asked me what I thought was the major difference between Zoomies and Grunts (ground Marines) on the ground.

I replied, "Zoomies are smart enough to march around mud puddles instead of through them and if we have our choice, we fly over them."

I worked hard at my duties and provided air support for many of the Battalion training exercises. Some were held in the northern training area of Okinawa and others held in Korea and Japan. I arranged air support to attack mock targets in support of Marines charging up hills, to directing transport-type aircraft by radio to drop supplies by parachute. I directed platoon-size paratroop drops and arranged for helicopter uses such as placing Marines in the front lines and medical evacuation flights.

My CO wanted to train the troops on the proper procedures for airlifting a Marine Company. I didn't want to ask the Air Wing in Japan to provide support because I thought it wasteful. The Marine Corps used C-119 aircraft, called flying boxcars, as transports. He didn't grasp the proper use of Marine Air support.

There are a series of bucket seats on both sides of the aircraft with seat belts. The boxcar rear ramp opens, the troops march in and sit down.

I thought it unnecessary training but knew better than argue with this particular CO since I was already on his shit list.

I requested the Air Wing provide two C-119 boxcars. I arranged a staging area alongside an off duty runway at Kadena Air Base.

The training consisted of the aircraft embarking and debarking the Marines after a short flight around the Island. Each Marine is considered on aircraft manifests weighing 250 pounds with full combat equipment.

A company of Marines arrived, about 180 men, commanded by Captain Dave Winfield. They stood at the parade rest position, a position between attention and rest, while briefed by Captain Winfield, a spit and polished, by the book Marine Officer. His uniform neatly pressed, belt buckle and boots glistened, looked like he stepped out of a recruiting poster.

Marine officers of the same rank who know each other use their first names. Dave Winfield was one of four Captains sharing my Quonset hut living quarters.

"Dave, the aircraft are on final approach and will taxi here shortly," I said.

"Fine, my troops are ready."

The two aircraft landed, taxied to our position and the pilot of the lead aircraft walked down the ramp.

As he approached, I recognized Captain John James. We flew in the same Squadron at

MCAS Cherry Point, NC when he was a fighter pilot.

John, a relaxed type, approached us wearing a crumpled sweaty flight suit, his cap sitting on the back of his head and flight shoes muddy and worn.

I knew this was trouble. There is no love lost between Marine Air and Ground Officers. Dave wouldn't appreciate his appearance, especially in front of his troops.

"Dave Winfield meet John James." I said.

"Hello, Captain," Dave said coldly.

"Hello, Captain," John answered.

"Do you have any questions about the flight?"

"Yes, Captain, how much weight can your airplane carry?"

"Well, Captain, I can carry 10,000 pounds for 1200 miles."

These guys are driving me nuts with all this Captain crap. They need to ease up.

"What I really want to know, Captain, is how many of my troopers can you carry?"

John got a smirk on his face. I knew he had enough of this guy.

"Captain, if you have one trooper who weighs 10,000 pounds, I can carry one."

I could hardly keep from laughing out loud.

After firing a couple of dirty looks between them, the training proceeded and uneventful for the remainder of the day.

AN ANGEL RODE MY WING

I maintained my aviation proficiency while stationed with the ground Marines and since my days were full with the Battalion, I flew mostly at night. I flew SNB Beechcraft aircraft out of NAS Naha, Okinawa located on the southern tip of the island. Fortunately, my brief stint as an instrument flight instructor back at Barin Field with the Navy came in handy while flying out of Naha.

The weather didn't always cooperate with my flight schedule. I used to take other Forward Air Controllers from other Battalions in the Regiment with me on several stormy night flights. One rainy, windy night I took a Lieutenant with me to get flight time and it was a particularly bad night to fly. He was my co-pilot and I flew an approach to Naha, directed by Naha's Ground Control Approach Radar when I told him we were in trouble because I wasn't wearing my Jewish Mezuzah, a small capsule worn on a chain around the neck. It has the Star of David on it and contains the ten Commandments. My aunt and uncle gave it to me when I entered flight training. I always wore it for luck when I flew.

"Don't worry," he said, "We are covered because I have my Saint Christopher Medal with me."

Good comeback, I thought.

We broke out of the clouds at 500 feet but still in a driving rainstorm and could barely see the runway ahead but managed to land safely. I will never know if it was my skill as a pilot or his

Saint Christopher Medal that got us home safely that night. Maybe a little of both.

BACK TO THE JETS

A4 Skyhawk

Upon completion of my Okinawan tour of duty and ordered back to MCAS Cherry Point, I joined Marine Aircraft Group-14 and was thrilled because they had three Attack Squadrons, all flying A-4 Skyhawks. Although trained as a jet fighter pilot and the Skyhawk. primarily an air-to-ground attack jet, I didn't care. I first saw the Skyhawk at NAS Naha on Okinawa the previous year and wanted to fly it. As an Air Liaison Officer and Forward Air Controller, I worked with A-4 pilots directing them by radio from the ground to find and destroy targets on the ground. At the end of the mission, I watched them climb toward the horizon in perfect formation and zoom toward their home base. I would then climb into my jeep. God, I felt jealous of those guys and determined to fly the A-4, given the opportunity, I could make it dance.

Having no immediate opening for me in an A-4 Squadron, I was assigned to a Marine Air Base Squadron as their executive officer, and able to fly the jets assigned to the Air Group, with the promise of an assignment to an A-4 Squadron as soon as available.

I got checked out in the F9F-8T Cougar jet, which I thought one of the most beautiful military jets ever built. It had a unique tail called a "flying" tail, the horizontal stabilizer mounted high up on the vertical stabilizer and the fuselage had straight bullet-like lines. It was designed as a fighter/attack plane and referred to as "the Grumman Iron Works" since it was a heavy airplane, built very solidly and very stable by the Grumman Aircraft Corporation.

As any fighter pilot knows, stability doesn't make for better fighter characteristics, actually, the more unstable an aircraft, the better a fighter plane. Stability tends to keep speed and direction the same, so if you put it in a bank, the aircraft initially wants to keep the same direction, while a more unstable aircraft will change direction quickly, which enhances it's fighter characteristics. I flew the Cougar for six months and finally got orders to join VMA-224, a Skyhawk squadron.

On June 10, 1960, I strapped myself into an A-4 Skyhawk, taxied out to the main runway at Cherry Point, lined up with the runway centerline and heard those magic words, "Cleared for takeoff."

I thrust the throttle forward and marveled at the acceleration, eased the stick back at 127 knots and felt it lift off and head for the sky for the first time in an aircraft that would be the major aircraft of my twenty year military flying career. I knew immediately this was the aircraft for me. It's like how you know what girl you want to ask to the Prom. You ask the one you really want to dance with. I really wanted to dance among the clouds with that airplane.

The Squadron Commanding Officer's handle was Barrel. I assumed from his barrel shaped chest. After I completed about a total of ten hours of training in the A-4, I found myself scheduled to fly a training flight on the Barrel's wing. I asked one of the Squadron pilots what it's like flying on the Skipper's wing. He told me to stay in tight and don't let him shake me off.

"When I look at my wing, I want to see you there," Barrel said, during the briefing for the flight in the ready room.

"Yes sir," I replied.

We took off and I immediately joined on his wing and hung in there nice and tight. We headed toward the practice aerobatic area. Once we arrived, we started a series of acrobatic maneuvers. He really tried to wring it out and shake me off. We kept getting lower and lower and did a few aileron rolls at just a few hundred feet above the ground.

So far, so good and then he dove down close to the ground, picked up speed and pulled the nose up to a forty-five degree angle and started a barrel roll. That maneuver takes much more altitude than a simple aileron roll. As we rolled inverted, I realized we were going to be very close to the ground at the bottom of the roll. I wondered if the Skipper made a mistake and started too low. I needed to make a quick decision either to abort the maneuver safely or stick to his wing and try to pull out at the bottom. I decided to bite the bullet and gut it out and go through with the maneuver. I stuck to his wing like glue. We had to pull real hard at the bottom and just missed the treetops by a few feet.

After landing, we walked in from the flight line. "Do you have any questions about the barrel roll?"

"No sir."

"All of my pilots can fly. I only want the ones with guts in my Squadron."

AN ANGEL RODE MY WING

I thought, what about that old pilot quotation that said, "There are old pilots and there are bold pilots, but there are no old bold pilots."

Barrel died since then, but it wasn't in an airplane.

COMBAT READY ATTACK SQUADRON

I was assigned to VMA-224 for only a few weeks when the Squadron deployed on a six-month Mediterranean cruise aboard an aircraft carrier. Wanting to go with them, I wasn't "combat ready" yet, so they transferred me to VMA-242, another Skyhawk squadron to complete my training.

My training went well and since VMA-224 deployed, our training accelerated so we qualified as a combat ready attack squadron in just a few months.

Shortly after our combat ready designation, we suddenly deployed to Puerto Rico. The Squadron Duty Officer called and told us to report to the Squadron by 1700 hours. We flew out at 0800 the next morning. Our personnel and equipment followed. That's the reason Marines live out of wooden boxes ready to go at all times. They just nail the lids on and put them on pallets.

AN ANGEL RODE MY WING

The entire squadron was in place at NAS Roosevelt Roads on the eastern tip of Puerto Rico by sundown the next day.

We were quickly briefed on the political and military situation and we were scheduled for combat air patrol flights starting early the following day.

I was scheduled to lead the first flight.

FLIGHT LOG-JUNE 5,1961
COMBAT AIR PATROL

We dragged ourselves down to the mess hall for a quick breakfast before our 0630 take off. It was 0545. The mess hall was closed, but one of our Marines swabbed the deck. I knocked on the glass door and motioned the Marine to let us in.

He did so with a cheery, "Good morning, sir."

I explained we needed a quick breakfast before we flew this combat mission. He went back to the kitchen and relayed my request to the Navy cook, a Chief Petty Officer. In those days, many Filipinos served with the Navy as cooks.

The Marine returned with the message from the cook the kitchen was closed. I quietly sent the Marine back to tell the cook I fully understood the kitchen was closed, but would he please cook us some eggs, bacon, toast and coffee and we would be on our way. The Marine again returned with the same message. I then went into the kitchen and explained to the cook that we needed breakfast before we flew.

"The kitchen is closed," he announced.

I grabbed his shirt collar, calmly removed my .38 caliber pistol from my shoulder holster and placed the muzzle right between his eyes.

"Do you cook breakfast for me and my men or do I blow your freakin' head off?"

"I'll cook it, I'll cook it."

After breakfast we took off.

When I returned from my flight, there was a message for me the Commanding Officer of the Naval Base wanted to see me and to report to his office immediately.

I entered his office. He glared at me and said he didn't appreciate me pulling a gun on his cook. I decided to use discretion and not correct him it was my weapon, not my gun as we Marines would say.

"If you were the Commanding Officer, what action would you take in a case like this?"

"If I was the Commanding Officer, I would open my kitchen earlier."

He bellowed, "Get the hell out of here and I don't ever want to see you again."

He never did.

There was political unrest on the Caribbean Island of The Dominican Republic. It was pretty serious stuff because all Americans on the island were ordered to evacuate. In order to carry off this evacuation our Marines landed. All went well except seven Americans were held hostage in a major hotel.

The captors stationed military units around the hotel.

Our Marines formed a perimeter around the hotel and called for overhead air support if needed to help complete the mission. This type of support is called "CAP" or combat air patrol.

I led a flight of four aircraft, early in the morning of the June 5, 1961. We circled overhead for a couple of hours without incident while our ground Marines rescued the Americans from the hotel.

THE FIASCO IN CUBA

The Squadron had another two-month deployment to Puerto Rico for training purposes in 1962. We practiced all phases of training out of NAS Roosevelt Roads. One of the training areas was the eastern half of a small island of Vieques, a few miles east of Puerto Rico. The Navy and Marine Corps recently stopped training there because it had become politically incorrect. It was a perfect place to simulate air cover during Marine landings or better known as "close air support" training.

We flew hard and often, day and night but when we didn't fly at night we partied at the Officer's club and listened to steel bands and consumed a lot of rum. After all, it was the Caribbean.

As often is the case, our Military units are deployed for training while something else is going on of a hostile political nature somewhere close by. In this case Castro threatened to invade the Naval Air Station at Guantanamo Bay, Cuba.

I was ordered to lead a flight of four A-4s to Guantanamo Bay and spend the rest of our deployment there. The Squadron sent eighteen men and the equipment to support flight operations for our four aircraft.

As four pilots, we flew two at a time practicing training flights such as dropping bombs and firing rockets. We each flew two of these flights during the day. While two of us zoomed the skies, the other two aircraft were fully loaded with ordnance and ready to carry out combat operations against Castro's forces if needed. All four of us flew all the way around the Island of Cuba each night just to show up on Castro's radar and let him know we were there to defend the fence line, which surrounded the base. The same fence line made popular during the movie called "A Few Good Men" where Jack Nickolson played a Marine Colonel whose primary duty was to defend the fence line and made the classic phrase, "You can't handle the truth," when told by Tom Cruise playing a Navy lawyer, "I want the truth."

We flew hard all day and when we finished at night we would mosey up to the O'Club bar and have a couple of cuba libres before hitting the sack. This went on for an entire month with hardly a word from the Squadron back at Roosevelt Roads. We really felt like outcasts from the Squadron. The jet field was across the bay from the main base making us isolated from any life outside of our duty. It was hard to keep our morale up but we were Marines so did our job well and didn't complain.

Finally, after a full month, we received orders to pack up and get ready to leave because the Squadron was returning to Marine Corps Air Station Cherry Point, NC, our home base, the next day. A C-130 transport flew in the next morning to fly the men and equipment of our detachment home.

My orders came to me in the form of a telegram from my CO to me personally.

It read, "The Squadron will pass the East Point of Cuba at 30,000 feet at 0930 tomorrow morning. You are to orbit the East Point designated point alpha at 32,000 feet and check in with the Squadron at 0930. You are not to leave point alpha until you have checked in on the Squadron frequency and the Squadron has passed that point." Point alpha was the eastern point of Cuba.

I read those orders very carefully and I found it interesting. Not only had the CO of the Squadron isolated us for a month, he didn't include us in the flight home. The orders didn't say anything about joining the Squadron for the flight home. It said don't leave until they passed.

Already pissed at him, I got a brainstorm and told my three wingmen unless he specifically told us to tail in behind him and join the Squadron, and knowing the CO would take the safe route to Miami and up the coast to Cherry Point, we would fly about 1200 miles directly over water to Cherry Point and beat the Squadron home.

With no precise orders after checking in, I headed my flight for Cherry Point directly over water and completely out of sight of land for a couple of hours.

We approached Point Lookout not far from Cape Hatteras, NC with plenty of fuel to spare.

I liked being a maverick.

We made a snappy break from our tight formation over the runway at Cherry Point and after we landed we taxied over to the Squadron flight line. It sure felt good to be home again. When I taxied as lead plane into the flight line area, I knew I was in trouble. I climbed out of my aircraft and was greeted by the Commanding General of the 2nd Marine Air Wing, the Cherry Point Marine Marching Band and the press. They took a picture of my family and me reuniting after two months.

WELCOME HOME—Capt. Hugh N. Levin, VMA-332's assistant operations officer, is swamped by family affection upon his return here from the Caribbean. On the "welcoming committee" were Capt. Levin's wife, Mary Alice, and three of their four children, Deborah, David, and Donna (standing). Dale, the youngest, was napping when his dad returned.

Welcome home

Of course, all of these things were intended for my Commanding Officer, who by all rights should have been taxiing the first aircraft into the Squadron area but I beat him home and came in first.

A couple of months later, I received orders, transferring me to Quantico, VA. to attend a six-month training course in Communications Officers School. Gee, I wonder why.

I happened to run into the CO a few years later after I matured a little and offered him my sincere apology.

He was a General then and still didn't like me.

THE CUBAN MISSILE CRISIS

In March of 1962, I attended the Marine Corps Communications Officers School at Quantico, Virginia for six-months. Here I was again, doing ground duty when all I wanted to do was fly. They had T-28s at their small airfield so I made many trips between Quantico and Norfolk to get in my flight time.

I hated going to class each day but I did make good friends and I learned a lot about all types of communications. The class was on a field trip in a wooded area of Virginia, when the Officer in Charge sent a few men and me by helicopter about ten miles forward from the main body to find a good spot to setup headquarters and establish communications with them. He would then hike in and locate the area I chose.

My men and I dropped into an open field. I found an area on the northern edge of the field in a lightly wooded area to establish the headquarters. When we completed the preliminary work and got established, I realized I had time to spare before the main body of the class arrived since they had to hike the ten miles. I took my helmet and pack off and lay down under the overhanging branch of a large tree. I rested my head on my pack like a pillow and was content to have the time to rest and just do nothing. I almost dozed off when a bird landed on the overhanging branch and dropped one right on my head. This has to be the lowest point of my career, I thought. Being an optimist, I figured things could only get better.

After graduating from the school, I went back to MCAS Cherry Point, NC for duty and assigned as Marine Aircraft Group 14's Communication Officer.

I immediately got involved in setting up the communications for a squadron making a trans-Atlantic crossing to Spain from Cherry Point. I went to Bermuda and conducted the communications between the C-130 aerial re-fueling tankers and the squadron's fighter planes. All went well and I got real good experience using single sideband radios capable of transmitting half way around the world. Bermuda was a nice place to be for a couple of weeks except for the hurricane that hit us.

I had been through a few hurricanes during my Marine career both in the States and in the Far East but when one hits you on a small island at full strength, it seems worse. We boarded up for a day until it passed. As I recall, Air Force nurses and civilian schoolteachers in the Women's barracks invited our small Marine contingent to a hurricane party. It seemed a better way to ride out a hurricane so we bought a couple of jugs of rum and joined them.

A C130 transport flew our equipment and us back to Cherry Point. As soon as I stepped off of the airplane ramp, I was informed the entire air group would leave for Key West, Florida early the next morning. I had just enough time to kiss the wife and kids and get a clean set of underwear.

We arrived at NAS Key West around noon the next day and I found myself going from the relaxed atmosphere of Bermuda to the tension of the possibility of a full scale war with Russia over their missiles placed in Cuba and pointed toward the United States.

As soon as I arrived, I set up the communications between all the fighter, photo and attack squadrons and communications with Air Force and Marine Commands and literally all the ships at sea. This all sounds easy but it took four days to complete especially laying miles of telephone wire. I knew my personal gear was on top of some cot somewhere in an old building set aside for the purpose of housing us. I never slept for the four days until my men and I completed the set up. I bought a new toothbrush and lived on hamburgers for four days. When I finally flopped on my cot, I slept for fourteen hours.

In typical fashion, the Marines lived under hardship conditions while the Air Force commandeered the Key West Holiday Inn.

I spent the rest of October 1962, either in the War Room at night or in the Group Headquarters during the day. I also spent time sitting in the cockpit of an A4 on the "Hot Pad." I was assigned duty to destroy the Cuban missile radar south of Havana, if and when ordered to launch.

The mission consisted of flying at an extremely low altitude just above the water, hitting landfall west of Havana then popping up, finding the missile site and destroying the radar with special ordnance called CBU, designed as a radar antenna and anti-personnel weapon. After completing the mission, the trick was to try to get the hell out of there in one piece. Naturally the area was very heavily defended. I got launched once but called back before I got to my first checkpoint.

Since I worked in the War Room, I had a crypto clearance, which is a step above top secret, so I was fully aware of the tense situation that existed between the United States and Russia. One of my jobs working in the War Room was to gather all intelligence data for the Commanding General's morning briefing.

I was proud of President Kennedy for holding his ground and calling Russia's bluff. When it was all over, President Kennedy came to Key West and commended us for being there and ready to fight.

He specifically commended VMCJ-2 as one of the Squadrons taking the famous pictures proving the missiles were there. The Air Force was also involved.

I had the honor of shaking his hand.

NUCLEAR WEAPONS
DELIVERY

Nuclear weapons delivery is the carrying and dropping of a nuclear or atomic bomb. I was a certified nuclear weapons delivery pilot. Earning the certification required six months of intensive training both in the air and ground school. After qualifying in all aspects of the training, the final certification came after a successful qualification flight called a check ride. This flight was conducted under the most stringent of rules and a nuclear pilot referee chased the flight in another A-4.

The qualification flight was designated A-20-R in the Marine jet attack training manual and my flight log shows two of these flights in my career.

The first was on February 7, 1962 and the other on June 11, 1965. The first qualified me as a nuclear delivery pilot and the second as one of seven Marine pilots chosen to be members of a contingency plan for a three-year period. Highly classified at the time, this plan if executed meant we would take off from a carrier, aerial refuel and drop nuclear weapons on designated targets. It has been almost forty years since that assignment has been de-classified, but I still don't feel comfortable discussing what the targets or what countries were involved, except to assure anyone who reads this, they were strictly military targets and involved no civilians or cities. It was also interesting there was no returning from the mission. If we survived the bomb blast and enemy fire we were to fly away from the target until we ran out of fuel and eject. Fortunately none of us ever had to fly the mission.

This isn't really about all that stuff anyhow and I only mention it to show the seriousness of the training for such a mission and the training that led up to the check ride. This part of the qualification requires me to fly what is called a "Sandblower" flight. It is flown at a very low level, not to exceed 200 feet above the terrain, from Cherry Point, across North Carolina, part of Virginia, into Kentucky, down to Tennessee where we popped up to 20,000 feet and met an air tanker C-130, aerial refueled and dove down to 200 feet again and proceeded across Alabama, Georgia to the coast and out to sea 100 miles, then south to a point 100 miles due east of Sanford, Florida.

At this point, I made a westerly run in to the coast to a checkpoint just north of Sanford and delivered the nuclear weapon to a target 25 miles inland. The weapon was the real thing except for the payload, which was 1000 pounds of TNT instead of nuclear material.

I mentioned this flight was flown under stringent rules. Points were deducted for being either 45 seconds early or late at any of many check points, 50 feet off of altitude, a half mile off of centerline on either side, meeting the tanker and aerial refueling at the proper place and time and using proper procedures to refuel, finding the target and delivering the weapon within 700 feet of it after tossing it to 14,200 feet in the air. Anything outside of the latter figures was disqualifying. The flight went fine and I qualified with a perfect score. It is not the flight but what happened during the flight I want to talk about.

I met the chase pilot referee in the ready room. He seemed like a nice enough guy, but I know that doesn't matter at all. These pilots are assigned by Wing HQ and it is their job to see that nobody slips through and gets qualified that isn't 100% ready.

I have checked the aircraft and the weapon over very carefully and now we are taking position for takeoff with two 300 gallon external fuel tanks, a full 5,200 pound fuselage tank and a bomb weighing 2,000 pounds or maximum gross weight of 22,500 pounds and a 10-knot tail wind. I have 10,000 feet of runway ahead of me and I will need all of it. Normally I would lift off at 140 knots but at this weight I need 170 knots and the tailwind will extend my take off run by 10%.

AN ANGEL RODE MY WING

Full throttle, I release the brakes and start the roll. Speed 110 knots and it really feels underpowered at this weight. 150 knots and half the runway is gone. I hope I figured this right. It is slowly accelerating now 160 knots and only 2,000 feet left. 170 knots and here comes the end of the runway, ease back the stick and hope she flies. Ahh, lift off and hell we had 100 feet left. Played it a little close, but we are on our way. All has gone as planned and I have the check point north of Sanford, Florida in sight so I pass over it at 50 feet and start my attack run at the target.

I'm over the checkpoint 100 % power and picked up speed to 615 mph and run 25 miles inland on heading 270 degrees to the target. The target is a circular clearing in the pines with a concrete blockhouse in the center of it. There are observers in a radio tower about a mile away while my chase plane watched my every move. I passed right over the target and start a 4g pull up, and hit the bomb release. The bomb will release when my nose position is past the vertical as it was preset to do. There it goes with a big kick of a foot ejector in the bomb rack. It's a powerful kick of 3,000 pounds of pressure. It actually jolts the aircraft.

That's when it happened. It kicked and I went completely dizzy. I couldn't seem to get my equilibrium steady and I felt sick in the stomach. The bomb hit less than 100 feet from the blockhouse so I was well qualified. Mission complete now all I had to do was get this thing home from Florida to North Carolina in one piece.

Neil Levin

I could hardly tell up from down and couldn't shake it off. I had a bad case of vertigo. Okay, climb to 25,000 feet and head for home. I put the plane on autopilot and fly using my instruments. I don't want the referee to know my condition because this is a check flight and I hope this dizziness will go away. I need to get on the ground though, so I call the chase plane and suggest we stop off at MCAS Beaufort, South Carolina and grab a bite to eat. He rogers that and I manage to somehow make a halfway decent landing at Beaufort. We grabbed a burger and coke at the snack bar and took a breather for about an hour. Feeling better, I suggest we take off for home.

As soon as I was airborne it happened again. The dizziness came back and I immediately put the airplane on autopilot. As we approached Cherry Point, North Carolina it really got bad and everything spun in my head. I had difficulty even reading my flight instruments and I almost forgot to mention that the last half hour of the flight was at night. I line up with the runway and lower the landing gear and flaps and slow to landing speed. Unfortunately doing that disengages the autopilot. Still real dizzy, I set up the landing attitude and hold the wings as level as I can and hold the throttle steady until I hit between the runway lights. I lost depth perception at this point. Drifting left so I correct to the right. Darn, I am drifting right too much. Got to keep it between the lights. There, I hit the runway and now just steer this thing straight. I feel better since I am on the ground but still dizzy.

84

AN ANGEL RODE MY WING

After I got out of the airplane I felt dizzy walking into the flight line shack and even had difficulty signing the aircraft maintenance log.

I went to the ready room and was debriefed by the referee who gave me an outstanding score for the flight. Of course I was stupid. I should have told him of my trouble and stayed at Beaufort but I was very proud and afraid that if I needed any medical attention I might be grounded and if it was serious it could mean the end of my flying career.

I called a flight surgeon friend of mine and he agreed to see me in the morning. He examined me and sent me to an eye, ear, nose and throat specialist. The specialist pulled wax plugs out of each ear and it was like caging a gyro.

I got all my balance and stability back and was fine after that. Evidently the jolt from dropping the bomb triggered the instability in my head by the wax causing unequal pressure on my inner ears and caused the dizziness.

I went on to fly many more nuclear training flights and in 1965, I received the 2nd Marine Air Wing Top Gun Award for Over the Shoulder Nuclear Weapons Delivery. But then that is another story.

MARINE ATTACK
SQUADRON 224

THE TOP GUN SQUADRON

A-4 Formation Flight

I accumulated a lot of flight time in the A4, and one day I was called into the Group Commanding Officer's office. I had no idea why he wanted to see me. I previously checked him out in the A4 and chased him on some of his early familiarization flights in another A4. The T-A4 or training version of the A4 with two seats wasn't available to us at the time.

It's unusual for a Marine Captain to be told to report directly to the Group Commander without going through his Commanding Officer. I stood at attention before his desk and he motioned me to sit down.

I couldn't believe what he said to me. I felt like I was a three-year-old kid who got his own ice cream wagon and candy store.

"Captain Levin, VMA-224 is being reassigned from Iwakuni, Japan to our air group," he said. "We will receive new A4s shortly and squadron personnel and equipment are being transferred now. I want you to form a squadron cadre and take over as the officer-in-charge. I want you to set up a training syllabus and personally oversee the training of new pilots as we form the new Squadron. A Lieutenant Colonel will be assigned in a few months and he will take over as the Squadron Commanding Officer. Until then you will be in command. Do you think you can handle that?"

I was completely overwhelmed and excited beyond belief. Even though it wouldn't officially become a Squadron until the Squadron Colors were passed to the new Commanding Officer, I would be in Command until then. I wanted to shout, "Colonel, you bet your sweet ass I can."

"Yes Sir, I can handle that," I answered quietly and calmly.

I didn't realize it then, but VMA-224 would be the most important Squadron in my twenty-year Marine flying career and it all started right then and there. For three and a half years, I went through complete combat training and my first of two combat tours in Vietnam. The Squadron was known throughout the Marine Corps and to the enemy as the "Top Gun Squadron." Along the way I would meet, befriend and fly with some of the best pilots in the Marine Corps. We had telltale green stripes in an arc painted on our tails.

A new Commanding officer arrived a few months later, but now that I had my first taste of Command, I knew I must attain the rank of Lieutenant Colonel and command a full-fledged Squadron someday. As it turned out later in my career, I did both of those things.

The Squadron formed well and the combat training kept right on schedule, when all of a sudden, in mid 1964 a different Commanding Officer was assigned. Soon the word was out. VMA-225 was getting ready to deploy to the Far East as the first Marine Squadron to go into combat in Vietnam. CO, Lieutenant Colonel Tom Mulvihill would lead VMA-224 into combat and relieve VMA-225. We needed his leadership and one who bonded us all.

AN ANGEL RODE MY WING

The first thing he told us was we would go into combat in Vietnam within a year. He only wanted volunteers and he gave us all the chance to transfer out. Nobody did.

He was the best Commanding Officer I ever had. I learned very much about leadership from him. I called him my mentor and I like to think later I became a better Commanding Officer because of some of the things I observed about him and learned from him.

We spent the next year training so when we got our first taste of combat, we were ready.

BASKET OF FRUIT

Ltcol. Mulvihill was unique in many ways. He didn't always handle things by the book and he had a deep sense of understanding.

At the time, assigned duty as the Squadron Aircraft Maintenance Officer, about 350 men were under my charge. We had three working shifts because aircraft maintenance is an around the clock work schedule.

A Sergeant, who will remain unnamed for obvious reasons, worked the night shift. He met a woman in Japan on a previous tour of duty at Iwakuni Air Base and married her. They lived in a small trailer close to our base. He needed to go home early one night and much to his amazement found his wife in bed with another man.

He kicked the man out, gathered some things and moved into the Enlisted Men's Barracks for a couple of days. He returned only to find she changed the lock and refused to let him in. He discovered she ran a nightly business at their home for the six months they lived there.

Approximately two months later, I received a call from Ltcol. Mulvihill telling me to bring the sergeant to his office. He didn't tell me why he wanted to see us.

The sergeant's wife had stormed into the CO's office and complained the sergeant moved into the barracks and wasn't supporting her or paying any attention to her. After listening to her for a half an hour scream and yell how she was mistreated, the CO got a pretty good picture about the happenings in the trailer and why the sergeant moved out.

The sergeant had an excellent Marine record except for this mess.

Ltcol. Mulvihill decided to personally confront the sergeant about these charges instead of ordering an investigation that could lead to possible disciplinary action.

The sergeant and I entered the CO's office and stood at attention in front of his desk.

"Stand easy," he said. "Sergeant, I spent about half an hour listening to your wife complain you aren't supporting her or paying any attention to her. Is this true?"

"Yes sir," replied the sergeant.

"Well, sergeant, I think I have a pretty good handle about what is going on here, but as your Commanding Officer, I must advise you that you have certain responsibilities. Capt. Levin informed me you do an excellent job as an aircraft mechanic and you are a good Marine, but you have both legal and moral responsibilities toward your marriage. Do you understand that sergeant?"

"Yes Sir."

"All right. Since she complains you don't pay any attention to her and don't support her, I suggest you do something to remedy that. Consider talking to the Chaplain about your marital problems. Meanwhile you might send her a basket of fruit once a month. That will be all. Dismissed."

As we left his office, I thought my God what an interesting way to handle a sensitive situation. He kept this off the books yet discharged his duty as Commanding Officer by confronting him.

He let the Marine work it out and kept the Marine Corps out of it.

FLIGHT LOG 5 FEB. 1964
TEST FLIGHT

A-4 Test Flight

One of my collateral duties involving flying was Group Test Pilot as one of the designated pilots to flight test aircraft after they had major repair, to ensure they were safe for the Squadron pilots to fly.

In the afternoon of the 5th of February 1964, the Repair Squadron called me to flight test an A4 attack jet. I suited up, went over to the Repair Squadron and looked over the aircraft maintenance logs of the aircraft to be tested. Much to my surprise, I noticed this aircraft hadn't been flown for fourteen months. It seems they had cannibalized this plane to keep other planes flying. This practice is highly illegal and since they got away with it for so long, they decided to get it flying again before they got caught. The engine was totally re-built and almost all of the electrical, hydraulic and fuel systems had been replaced. I figured I better check it out pretty well.

I gave the aircraft a thorough preflight inspection both outside the aircraft and in the cockpit. The only thing unusual was the elevator portion of the tail was level instead of elevated eleven degrees. This is to reveal a panel that lets the pilot see the hydraulic fittings are connected to the flying tail. I couldn't see the panel.

I will attempt to recall the things thought and felt during this test flight.

I have full power, airspeed up and lift off. Controls feel good except the tail feels a little heavy. Trim out the trim tab to take pressure off of the tail. That tab is really sensitive. It feels like it moved the whole elevator instead of just the trim tab. I better have it fixed when I return so let's write it down on my kneeboard. I climbed to 42,000 feet and performed all of the initial checks on the aircraft. So far, so good. I switch to manual fuel control and bypass the altitude compensator on the fuel control. Ram accelerate the engine to maximum power. It's fine, so I switch back to automatic fuel control.

Here comes the fun part, here we go.

I roll this baby upside down and pull the nose down into a vertical dive and see how she handles after we break the sound barrier. Maximum power and straight down dive....8 mach .9 mach .956789—1.0 mach.

It always amazes me whenever I break the sound barrier how the aircraft vibrates going into it and after coming out of it, but how smooth the aircraft flies after breaking it.

We just passed through 35,000 feet, 30,000 feet and now at 25,000 feet we need to recover from this dive and be out of it by 10,000 feet.

Oh my God, the stick is frozen stiff. I can't move it. Of course you can't move it you idiot. It all comes to me now from the way the tail acted after takeoff and climb out.

The tail is not connected hydraulically and I am flying by wire.

I can't move the tail because at this speed of 1.2 mach I'm just not strong enough to overcome the tremendous pressure on the tail. Throttle back to idle and lock my legs and knees. Grab the stick with both hands and pull with all of my might.

10,000 feet and still going straight down.

Can't eject at this speed or I will literally be torn apart in the air. The nose inches slowly upward. Keep pulling. I have speed brakes but I

95

will only use them as a last resort. When the speed brakes are activated, the nose pitches up. Normally the flying tail compensates for this pitch up, but the flying tail is not connected. At this speed it will put about 11 or 12 gs on the aircraft. This means that the aircraft and I will weigh 11 or 12 times what we normally weigh in a split second. This will almost assuredly knock me unconscious at a time when I need to be awake to recover from this dive.

The nose is still slowly rising but I'm passing through 2,000 feet and still in too steep of a dive.

Must slow down to recover. This is it.

I must use the speed brakes and pull the stick with all my might. Brakes open now.

I am losing consciousness.

Well, I woke up at 12,000 feet and have no idea how I got here. The aircraft is rolling into another dive. I take over the controls and head for home. The wing looks wrinkled like a prune. The "g" meter indicates 11 gs. No wonder the wings are wrinkled. They were over stressed. Let's call MCAS Cherry Point tower and declare an emergency and fly straight in for a landing.

I am going to have a tough time explaining this one, but at least I came back. I sometimes think I lead a charmed life.

I did this day.

AIR GROUP DUTY OFFICER

Marine Corps captains were assigned Group Duty Officer watch about once every six weeks mainly being available for twenty-four hours handling minor problems for the Air Group CO and his staff. Things like taking complaint calls from parents living close to the base because their children can't sleep with the jet noise.

There was very little to do at night because most air operations shut down by eight pm.

One evening while on Group Duty, completely bored I decided to look at the Blue Book listing all officers in the Marine Corps with things like full name, serial number and date of rank I was curious about the full name of Captain Daniel P Parker. Dan Parker sounds like an all American name but what did the middle initial P stand for and why was he so secretive about it?

I looked him up and found the P was for Pufpaf.

Daniel Pufpaf Parker. I wondered why parents would name their son Pufpaf.

A short while later I got a call from the Havelock, NC Sheriff's Deputy. Havelock is a small town located just outside the Cherry Point Marine Base. He was holding one of our Marines for public drunkenness and was willing to turn the matter over to the Marine Corps.

I thanked him and assured him we would have a Marine MP pick him up shortly. The Marine was a corporal assigned to VMA-331, one of the attack squadrons in the air group.

I called VMA-331's Squadron Duty Officer.

"VMA –331 Squadron Duty Officer Lieutenant Pospisel speaking sir."

The strange sounding name caught me by surprise.

"You gotta be kidding me. Is your name really Pospisel?" I asked.

"Yes Sir."

"How do you spell that."

"P-o-s-p-i-s-e-l."

I ordered him to send an MP to the Sheriff's office to pick up his Marine and handle any disciplinary action within his squadron.

Wow, two strange names tonight. Pufpaf and Pospisel.

What if Lieutenant Pospisel's first name was Captain Parker's middle name?

Pufpaf Pospisel. Now there's a name.

Suppose his wife's name was Penelope?

They would be introduced at social events as Lieutenant Pufpaf and Penelope Pospisel.

Now going a step further, while attending a dog show for their poodle Pierre, they now would be introduced as Lieutenant Pupaf and Penelope Pospispel and poodle Pierre.

What a boring job this group duty is. I must find something more constructive to do than look up names in a Blue Book, I thought.

A few weeks later while flying over Norfolk, Virginia I had some minor engine problems and made a precautionary landing at Norfolk Naval Air Station. The maintenance crew needed to order a part and couldn't repair the plane until the next day so I checked into the BOQ, cleaned up and went to the O'Club dressed in my flight suit.

I chose a bar stool next to a visiting US Army captain and we had a few drinks and swapped stories.

I told him the Pospisel story and he laughed.

"That would be a funny name," he said, "however, not as funny as my Army friend Captain Muckinfuch."

FLIGHT LOG 20 JUNE 1964
NIGHT CARQUAL

Most people don't know it but Marine pilots are Naval Aviators and, as such, part of their combat readiness training is aircraft carrier operations. In order to qualify, a carrier pilot must complete six day and night landings. This training usually takes about a month when nearly all of the flying is practicing carrier landings under the watchful eye of a Landing Signal Officer or LSO. This practice takes place either at home base or some designated airfield a short flight away.

I qualified on land as did most of the squadron and all but one of us qualified, which means we successfully landed our A4 jet attack plane six times aboard the aircraft carrier CVA-60, The USS SARATOGA. The landings certainly were exciting but after practicing for a month, it was almost a let down after qualifying. It seemed easy to me. We flew a tight pattern around the ship at 800 feet and with good guidance from our LSO, we made trapped landings, snagging a cable on the deck of the ship with our tail hook, bringing us to an abrupt, putting it mildly, stop.

Up to the moment: It is 3AM on the morning of June 20, 1964. Instead of me being all cuddled up in bed like most of the rest of the people in the United States of America, I'm sitting in the cockpit of an A-4 attached to the starboard steam catapult on the bow of the USS Saratoga, one hundred miles off of the coast of Jacksonville, Florida.

We couldn't have picked a blacker night to qualify for night landings. No moon, overcast and a light rain with poor visibility. I can think of lots of places I would rather be, but I am here and the catapult officer signals to me. He's ready to launch me into the black night sky. I must admit, even though I have done this before in other airplanes and other jet airplanes, I'm a little nervous. Hell, this is downright scary.

Push the throttle to full power, stay off the brakes, grab handle to hold the throttle forward during the launch, pull the stick full back, brace legs, back, head and neck.

Ready! Salute the catapult officer to show him you are ready.

Here we gooo!!

In the air in a couple of seconds, 150 knots, wheels up, flaps up and establish a climb. Boy, let's keep this thing climbing. In pitch-black night with no visible horizon, we climb using our instruments. Here we are at 1500 feet and the ship's

101

tower directs us to descend to 1200 feet and turn left on a cross leg to a heading of 350 degrees. Okay, done.

We cruise at 250 knots and are instructed to turn further left to 170 degrees and maintain 1200 feet. Roger that! We pass abeam of the ship in the opposite direction.

Boy, it not only looks smaller at night, you can't see it at all. All you see is the centerline lights. They instructed us to turn and intercept our final leg and we will be 5 miles astern of the ship at 1200 feet.

Slow down, drop landing gear, half flaps and the tail hook. The lights of the ship are just a dot now. We checked in with the LSO and called hook and "ball," informing him our tail hook is down and we can see an amber light reflected off of a concave mirror reflected at an optimal landing angle and a bright amber in color. This light is referred to by pilots as the "meatball" or just "ball." Keep it centered up and down and in the middle from right and left all the way to touchdown on the deck of the ship.

Here we go, the ball is centered and we are on course. Drop full flaps and slow to 137 knots or about 160 miles per hour. Descend at a rate of descent of 500 feet per minute.

"You're looking good," says the LSO.

I'm sure glad he can see me because I can't see anything except the ball and the centerline lights.

"Okay, keep her coming down. Don't get too fast on me," he says. "Dip a little left, not too far, straighten out, keep her coming just like that, perfect glide angle, good speed, looking good at the fantail. Cleared to land."

Hold her steady, line up with the centerline lights and land right on them. Wheels touched down, now add full throttle in case we get a hook skip so we can get airborne again before we run out of deck space. The hook caught the number three wire or cable, the perfect one to catch. We are thrown forward as the cable rapidly decelerates us. We stop on the deck.

WOW, what a great feeling. What a RUSH!

Now all we have to do is taxi forward to the catapult and do it all over again five more times tonight.

TOP GUN

Our Squadron, VMA-224 entered competitive exercises along with other Marine Corps Attack Squadrons from January to June of 1965. Called Compexes, they were designed to test the combat readiness of both individual attack pilots and Attack Squadrons and were monitored and scored by referees in chase planes and on the ground in bunkers close to the targets, or on boats or barges when the target was on the water. There were specific rules for Compex flights. They were different for each type of attack delivery. For example, the rules for Compex rockets, you made five runs starting at exactly 7000 feet at a tank on the rocket range. The best and worst scores from these runs were thrown out and they averaged the scores from the remaining three runs and that would be your individual rocket compex score.

Actually, we competed in fifteen Compex Exercises and our Squadron, VMA-224 won all fifteen. Our pilots won "Top Gun" awards for their individual efforts. I won one for "over the shoulder nuclear weapons delivery" and another one for " pop-up bombing."

Ironically, I was shot down the following year in actual combat while executing a pop-up bombing run on a bridge, highway and railroad complex in North Vietnam, but not before I completely destroyed the target. This bridge complex was critical to the enemy's supply line.

The "special weapons" or nuclear weapons delivery top gun award was to me the most coveted because of the difficulty. It takes six months to train, many hours of ground school and many flights all under the watchful eye of referees and very little room for any mistakes. They involve low-level flights, high-level flights, aerial refueling, long distance navigation and four basic types of delivery.

After all the compex flights were flown, the final compex came down to two pilots, me and my Commanding Officer, Col. then Ltcol. Tom Mulvihill. We were tied for the Top Gun award in special weapons and the fly-off consisted of two bombs dropped by each of us on a barge in a bay twenty-five miles inland from the outer banks of North Carolina. Good friends and very competitive, we both wanted to win.

We briefed in the ready room and shook hands as we left for our aircraft. We nodded out of respect for each other, never wishing the other good luck or anything. He won the coin toss and chose to make his runs first. He led the flight out to the target area where we checked in with the referee. He kissed off to me and broke off from the formation and headed out to the outer banks to start his first run. I flew a wide orbit over the target. He flew a low level run right over the target on his first delivery. BULLS EYE!! He was no dummy. He knew he excelled at low level runs and wanted to put pressure on me. What he didn't realize was I excel under pressure. I made my run. BULLS EYE! We were still tied.

It all came down to the final delivery, the most difficult and least accurate. Hell, all you have to do to qualify is to drop the bomb within 1,400 feet of the target. You got a Navy "E" for excellence if you dropped the bomb within 700 feet of the target. Called the "over the shoulder delivery," you fly over the target and then pull up into the first part of a loop, tossing the bomb up at a pre-set and pre-determined angle set to release automatically. You pull up to 7000 feet and are now upside down. You perform the last half of a" half Cuban eight" maneuver where you dive for the deck inverted, roll right side up and fly away from the bomb blast at a very low altitude, like 50 feet at max power and speed. The bomb meanwhile goes up to 14,200 feet if your speed was right and then drops down on the target. Your accuracy depends on how steady and smoothly you perform the maneuver.

There he goes making his final run. He looks real good and I think he will drop the bomb pretty close to the target. There is his splash. The referee calls "50 feet."

"Okay, Levin, beat that for all the marbles," he quipped.

"I will. Watch," I retorted.

Here we are over the outer banks and 25 miles from the target. Speed up to max and we fly at 50 feet over the bay.

Don't think about what we have to beat, just think about hitting the target. I sense a right cross wind so I adjust my flight path to the target by 150 feet to the right. In other words, I will pass by the target at 150 feet to the right of it instead of directly over it to compensate for the wind. Here comes the target, pull up exactly 4gs and maintain level wings. This is real important when you consider what effect being just one degree off would do to a bomb's flight path that is being tossed up to 14,200 feet and then drops down again.

There goes the bomb being kicked off of the bomb rack according to our preset angle. It is kicked off with 3000 pounds of foot pressure. It's on its way and I pull upside down on the top of my loop. Heading down to the deck at max speed but I can't stand the suspense and I must see the bomb hit. We break off the escape run and bank hard toward the target. Here it comes and it is going to be real close. Am I seeing right? Yes! The referee confirms it. BULLS EYE!

Not a word from the CO. I join on his wing at 10,000 feet for our return flight to Cherry Point.

What is this? He is passing me the lead and joining on my wing. Now he is saluting me! He never was much for words but that gesture said it all.

Our Squadron was named the "TOP GUN" Squadron as a result of these Compexes. I was always proud to have helped with that honor, as were many other pilots in the Squadron. What is more important, however, is the Squadron was obviously well trained and combat ready. I must admit though, actual combat is a lot different than these structured compex exercises. When someone is shooting at you, scores aren't very important.

SOMETHING SPECIAL

I would like to digress a little and go back to something that happened while helping to train the new Squadron. As a designated test pilot, I just returned from a test flight and landed back at Cherry Point, our home base and taxied into the flight line. I climbed out of the cockpit and saw that the flight line Marine had a very somber look on his face. I gathered my gear and walked into the flight line shack to sign the "yellow sheet" or aircraft maintenance log and noticed that all the Marines had a somber look on their faces. Something was up.

It was late in the afternoon of November 22, 1963. The flight Line Sergeant told me that President Kennedy had been shot and killed. That is where I was at the time. If you are over forty-five, you probably know where you were too.

THE COP CAR CAPER

Hey, remember the night Pete got in the cop car?

It's a requirement for pilots to maintain proficiency in cross-country navigation flights, meaning fly to an airport other than home base, land and return.

I flew to McCoy Air Force Base in Orlando, Florida with Pete Booher, a fellow pilot in VMA-224. We flew together often and formed a close friendship that exists today. Pete is a good-looking guy, with muscular build still in great shape, close-cropped hair, and even after spending many years as a Western and Delta Airline captain, he is still a Marine's Marine. You couldn't ask for a more loyal friend. We not only flew together, we played golf, went to happy hour and generally hung out together. When we were late coming home from happy hour, his wife blamed me and my wife blamed him.

AN ANGEL RODE MY WING

We flew two A4 Skyhawks from MCAS Cherry Point, NC to McCoy. A beautiful clear Friday afternoon, we cruised south along the coast with over one hundred miles visibility. South Carolina, Georgia and Florida looked just like the map.

McCoy AFB shared half the field with Orlando International Airport and as Marines, we wanted to look sharp entering their traffic pattern. We passed over the runway like the Blue Angels do in tight formation at the proper altitude and speed for military aircraft and entered their landing pattern with a snappy left break from each other, followed by a tight turn to the downwind leg.

We taxied to their flight line together and noticed numerous flying Constellations based there. The Constellation was a multi-engine prop transport plane with a tri-tail. We learned later, the center tail was cosmetic and had no aeronautical value.

We secured our aircraft, checked into the BOQ, changed into civilian clothes and walked to the Officers Club.

We arrived to a full swinging Happy Hour. Pete and I found a good spot at the bar and ordered drinks. Air Force pilots made gestures with their hands representing flight maneuvers. The hand maneuvers got more intense as the evening wore on and the booze flowed. Pete and I looked at each other and burst out laughing.

"What's so funny?" an Air Force pilot asked.

"Hell, you guys are funny." I replied. "We're Marine attack pilots and it seems funny to us that you transport guys with funny looking tails on your planes are making all the gestures."

After a heated argument about whether the Air Force or Marine Corps had better pilots, they extended the welcome mat and bought us drinks. We reciprocated with a couple rounds. It's a good thing drinks are cheap at Happy Hour.

After we all became buddies, one of them suggested we go with them to a Young Republicans Club party in Orlando. Neither Pete nor I cared what politics were involved. A party is a party. Let's go.

The party was at a small house crowded with wall-to-wall people, mostly young Republicans on the outskirts of Orlando. Pete settled down in the living room. I pushed my way through to the kitchen, got a rum and coke and went out on the back porch where I could move around and talk to people.

I was talking to a good-looking young Republican when the stereo played the Cha-Cha. The timing was perfect since my dance instructor friend, Syd showed me a few basic and some not so basic Cha-Cha steps recently. It was the latest and hottest dance at the time. I got popular real fast and spent the next two hours teaching lovely young Republican ladies how to Cha-Cha. Of course, I had a few more rum and cokes between dances.

I wondered where Pete was. An absolutely gorgeous gal came out on the porch and told me my buddy Pete was passed out in the living room chair. Pete and I always look after each other so I needed to find a way to get him out to the Air Force base and let him sleep it off.

The gorgeous gal offered to take us close to the base. She dropped us off at an all-night diner and we went in for some coffee and to call a cab. I left Pete at the lunch counter while I called a cab from the rest room.

Gone only a few minutes, I returned and Pete was gone. Two cops sat at the end of the counter having coffee. I looked outside for Pete and found him in a most unusual place in the back of the cop car.

"Pete get the hell out of there," I said. "C'mon Pete, this isn't funny."

He slowly lifted his head and turned toward me.

"Get in the freakin' cab," he said.

"It's not a cab. It's a cop car."

"It's a cab."

"Pete, it's not a cab, it's a cop car."

I sensed someone standing behind me. I turned. The two cops had their heads cocked and their hands on their hips with a look like my Mother used to have when she caught me with my hand in the cookie jar.

"Officer, I called a cab and my buddy thought this was it," I said. "We're just trying to get out to the base after a party. We are not driving."

"Get him out of our car and into a cab and go straight to the base. No stopping anywhere."

"Yes sir!"

We slept it off that night and flew back to Cherry Point the next day.

This little story has followed Pete around for years.

It always starts with "Hey, remember the night Pete got in the cop car?"

THE WAR YEARS

CHU LAI—SOUTH VIETNAM

THE DOOR

After an exhausting flight from Travis Air Force Base on an Air Force jet transport, we, the main body of our Squadron VMA-224, milled around in the terminal at Clark Air Force Base in the Philippines. We waited for some Air Force C-130 turbo-prop planes to take us the remaining 750 miles into South Vietnam. The advance party of the Squadron was already there. We stopped briefly on Hawaii and made another brief stop for refueling on Wake Island. Wake Island is so small the runway took up most of the space on it.

Knowing it will be about a four and a half hour wait before we leave, gave me plenty of time to reflect on where I have been, where I am and where I am going.

Neil Levin

The Squadron trained well to prepare for combat. We weren't known as the Top Gun Squadron for nothing. Most of us had been flying together in this squadron for one and a half to two years so we were ready, at least on paper.

You are never ready for combat until you are there.

I looked through a glass door out onto the concrete apron where the C-130s are parked. We will go through that door and the transports will fly us directly across the South China Sea to Chu Lai, South Vietnam.

It occurred to me this is the last normal civilization I will see before going into War. As I looked around, I watched people coming and going. Some buy tickets with airlines to fly them back home to the States. Others meet and greet people arriving either from leave or to be stationed at Clark Air Force Base.

I look through the side glass wall of the terminal at the commissary across the street. Many Air Force families are stationed here at Clark and their life goes on in a normal manner as we pass through. Wives arrive at the commissary in their small cars. Some carry small babies, some had little kids going inside with them as they did their grocery shopping. I wonder if I will ever see my kids again. Those wives will have dinner with their husbands tonight while I go through that glass door.

It's as if I will leave one time zone and enter a different world. The people here don't have survival or combat as priorities on their mind. For them it is more like "What's for dinner?" Once I go through that door, my life will change until I go through a door again on my way home after the scheduled thirteen months from now. That is if I am lucky enough to go home.

We now approach the coast of South Vietnam. It is mountains, jungle and beautiful secluded beaches. The water along the beaches is bright green in color and so clear you can see the bottom and the coral reefs. I can see Chu Lai now that will be my home for over a year. It is very sandy with a short runway and lots of tents near the beach and more tents along the flight line. The flight line had walled revetments, each with an A4 parked in it to protect the planes from enemy mortar, rocket and satchel charge attack.

We landed and parked at the operations platform. The tailgate ramp of the C-130 is lowered and I am hit in the face with a blast of unimaginable heat of at least 120 degrees. I walked down the ramp and put my feet on the soil of Vietnam for the first time. It is October 1965. What will happen to me and what will I do here between now and November 1966?

I keep thinking about that glass door back in the terminal at Clark AFB and I now realize that for me it wasn't a door at all. It was the passageway to a completely different life.

SOME FUNNY STUFF

In Chu Lai, we lived in tents with two things outside. One was a foxhole to dive into during the enemy mortar and rocket attacks and the other a rocket tube buried three quarters in the sandy soil. This tube, called a rocket pod, once held nineteen aerial rockets. After the rocket pods served their usefulness, we used them as urinals. There were no women at Chu Lai and also no restroom facilities so we fend for ourselves. There was a shack called a four holer we could go to but it was quite a distance from my tent. It was more convenient to use the rocket pods.

It was the middle of the night when the mortar attack started. Mortars made a screeching sound in the air and a loud crackling when they hit, while rockets made a whine in the air and a whump when they hit. You could actually see them coming. These were mortars. Benny and I, in our skivvies with our flak jackets and steel helmets, dove out the side flap of the tent into our shallow foxhole. Benny was one of my three tent mates. We had our .38 caliber pistols drawn in case the enemy charged into our complex during the mortar attack. All hell was blowing up around us while Benny and I pushed our bodies as deep as we could into the foxhole.

"Benny," I shouted.

"What?"

"If we live through this, let's dig this damn foxhole deeper in the morning."

The next morning Benny and I dug that foxhole so deep we had to practically help each other out of it. All the guys who had warned us about our shallow foxhole stood around and laughed.

My tent and the rocket pod were right next to the road. Well, not really a road, more like a path with jeep tracks in it. I was standing at my rocket pod, relieving myself when a jeep came along. I didn't pay any attention to it because there were no women at Chu Lai and the whole place was like a big urinal anyhow. I happened to look up as the jeep passed and low and behold, there was Martha Raye, the comedian, singer, entertainer, sitting in the back of the jeep.

She smiled, waved at me and said, "Hi Marine."

"Hi," I said, but was so embarrassed I wanted to climb into the rocket pod.

She was in Vietnam to entertain the troops. Her plane made a re-fueling stop at Chu Lai and she was on her way to our mess tent to have lunch with the troops, which she loved to do.

Neil in Chu-Lai

One day about ten years later, I walked into a bar in Laguna Beach, California and there was Martha Raye sitting at the bar by herself. I sat on the bar stool next to her and told her that we had met once before. When I told her about it, she remembered the incident and she laughed. She then bought me a martini for old times sake.

BIG RED

We didn't exactly have many comforts of home at Chu Lai. No flushing toilets or running water in our quarters. We lived in tents on the sand at first and later they built wooden flooring. We each had a cot and a wooden crate standing on end as a shelf and table for our personal stuff like shaving cream, toothpaste and soap. We hung our knife and .38 caliber pistol on nails on the side of our crate right within our reach as we slept at night. We always kept a flashlight on our makeshift table. If we had to go to the bathroom at night, we took our knife, pistol and flashlight with us. As we walked along, we whistled or sang to let the sentries know we were not a Viet Cong that managed to sneak into the compound. There were many sentries behind many trees but you never saw them. They had blackened faces and were camouflaged. Every once in a while they shot a Viet Cong who tried to sneak into our tents.

I had one comfort none of the others in my tent did. I flew a plane to Japan for special modifications and brought a fan back. Many times as I left the tent to fly a mission in North Vietnam, one of the guys jokingly asked for my fan if I didn't come back. Actually, I did get shot down in North Vietnam and one of the guys took my fan as a joke before I returned after being rescued.

Anyhow, I got through another night in paradise and stood outside of my tent where I had my own five-gallon water can. I was shaving out of my helmet early in the morning when I spotted movement in the bushes behind me in my tin mirror.

I turned prepared to face the enemy and stared at a three-foot red iguana.

His tongue flashed.

Christ, now what? I thought.

I reached into my tent flap and grabbed my pistol and a can of peanuts. Fortunately for him, I tried the peanuts first. I threw a few peanuts to him and he liked them. He went away but returned the next morning. This time I threw them closer to where I stood and he came to them.

I went down to our little PX and bought six cans of peanuts. It occurred to me that things must be pretty tough when I'm so lonely I try to make friends with a small dragon.

He came around each morning and eventually he trusted me enough to eat peanuts out of my hand and I trusted him to not bite the hand that feeds him. I looked forward to his visits and he became my buddy. I dubbed him, Big Red.

NOT FUNNY STUFF

A MATTER OF DISCIPLINE

While I was at Chu Lai, other countries had troops also like Australia, Turkey and South Korea.

My tent was near the beach and about a block away from the flight line. Although we had flight operations going on around the clock seven days a week, this was one of those rare nights I wasn't scheduled to fly.

I was in my tent playing a friendly game of cards with a South Korean Major, the Commanding Officer of the South Korean troops. It was their job to protect part of the airfield from infiltrating Viet Cong. Our own Marines were responsible for overall security but our allies helped them out.

The Major's Top Sergeant came into the tent and said something to the Major in Korean.

AN ANGEL RODE MY WING

The Major excused himself, saying he had to take care of something and wouldn't be long.

When he returned about twenty minutes later, he looked a little disturbed.

"Is everything all right?" I asked.

"Yes," he replied. "I had to discipline one of my men for falling asleep on sentry duty."

"How did you discipline him?"

"I shot him in the head."

SHOT DOWN—TALLY HO

LOG BOOK ENTRY 21 JULY 1966

Tally Ho was the code name for aerial combat missions flown over North Vietnam. I led a flight of four A4 Skyhawk Attack Jets over North Vietnam on July 21, 1966. After destroying a bridge over a river for two major highways and a railroad track, my aircraft was shot down by enemy anti-aircraft fire. Probably one or more 155 mm cannon rounds hit me. Although I am writing about this over thirty years later, my thoughts about what happened that day are crystal clear in my mind as if locked up all that time and time to release them. The following are my thoughts about what turned out to be one of the most nerve wracking days of my life.

I tried to pump up my wingmen with the following. "Okay, guys," I said, "We were briefed by intelligence and this is no easy target. Six aircraft from the Air Force and the Navy were shot down in three days and three pilots have been killed, trying to destroy this bridge. Needless to say, it is very heavily defended. One of our Marine flights tried this morning and reported enemy anti-aircraft guns surrounded the target and with extremely heavy flak. They missed the target. Keep alert and follow my lead. Are we ready? Let's go get it."

We are airborne. God, I love this. Climbed to 20,000 feet and skirted around the DMZ, the Demilitarized Zone. We are now over North Vietnam and heading toward the target area. Twenty miles from the target and diving for the deck. Full throttle, maximum speed over 615 mph, tree top level, on course to the target.

"Step up on my wing, guys, I don't want any of you hitting a tree."

Funny thing, here we are, each carrying six 500-pound bombs and we are so low a kid could knock us out of the air by tossing his lunchbox up. Got to stay low. Our best chance of getting through the enemy defenses is to completely surprise them.

My wingmen hang in there good and tight. I spread them out into combat formation just before we pop-up at the target. So far, so good. There's the river checkpoint just ahead.

"Spread out and pop-up to 7,000 feet on my signal. Arm bombs.... "Pop-up now. Attack! Attack!"

At 7,000 feet and there it is—dead ahead. Jeez, I could almost walk on all this flak. Keep going, roll inverted hard, target in the bombsite and pull hard into dive on the target.

Dive, dive, 3,500 feet and bombs away. Pulled out of dive with hard pull up and to the right and got a glimpse of the target. Got it dead center. The bridge is completely destroyed. There is a huge hole. The mid section of the bridge is gone with nothing but twisted steel left on both sides.

Call off wingmen quickly before somebody gets hit. There is no need for them to dive on a destroyed target. Keep aircraft moving away from the target area. Don't give them an easy target. Tracer shells zipped all around me. Pull hard and keep jinking. Moving rapidly from side to side by constantly reversing course and climb.

Pow!

Real heavy thud rocked the aircraft. I'm hit bad. The entire jet intake just behind the right side of the cockpit is completely gone. Just jagged metal left.

Also a pain in my right side above the hip. I took some shrapnel. Bleeding but not bad. Just a nick.

Smoke filled in the cockpit. Real thick now. Open the air vent and blow it out. Tailpipe temperature is over red line at 1,000 degrees centigrade. Maximum for the engine is 650 degrees centigrade.

"You are on fire. Eject! Eject!" wingmen scream.

AN ANGEL RODE MY WING

Still climbing. I gave a radio distress Mayday call with my position and sent my wingmen home before they get too short of fuel to make it. All of my training says to eject before this thing becomes a fireball and explodes. If I do and I make it safely to the ground, I will probably become a prisoner of war. If I can make it to the Gulf of Tonkin about 25 miles from here I might have a chance to escape capture.

Hell, I'm going for it.

Still together and five miles out over the Gulf. It's getting real hot in here and the engine is gone. I have to get out now. Pull the curtain over my face and brace my back and lock my legs and feet.

Wow, what a kick in the pants. I tumble over and over. There goes the seat falling away from me and I'm free falling. I ejected at 16,000 feet and the chute should open automatically at 10,000 feet so I have to fall a mile. Grab the ripcord handle in case it doesn't open automatically and open it manually, if necessary.

There, it opened. My God, look at my plane. It's just a fireball. It looks more like a comet burning up in the atmosphere. It exploded apart before it hit the water.

Looks like I guessed right about the time to get out of there. Gee, it's so quiet up here. Before I start to like this, I better pay attention to what is happening. I must have a 35-knot wind, blowing me back toward land and the enemy. Not only that but there are two enemy patrol boats coming out after me. My God, they are shooting at me while I dangle in this parachute. Okay, if they want a fight, they're going to get one. Take out radio pack and call for help. Got two Air Force and two Navy planes responding to my call. Remember your forward air control training from when you served with the ground troops on Okinawa and use it now.

Ah, there they are. Give them headings to fly to my area and direct them with left and right turns toward the two gunboats. They have the enemy boats spotted.

I am getting lower and closer to the gunboats and the firing is more intense. The aircrafts are diving and firing at the gunboats just in time.

They blew the boats right out of the water. The lousy bastards got what they deserved for shooting at Mrs. Levin's little boy in a parachute.

I am down to about 500 feet above the water. Hook my raft lanyard to my harness to secure it to me and pull the handle to blow the raft to full size. The raft was folded neatly and attached to my parachute seat pack. When I pulled the handle it released carbon dioxide from a capsule similar to blowing up a spare tire stored in your car trunk. Funny how often I complained about having to go through this type of training over and over again during my aviation career. All of a sudden, it's all worth it.

Now what? Sharks everywhere. I hope they were right when they said the sharks were just as afraid of us. Well, I have my knife, my pistol and some shark repellant. They are standard equipment when we fly combat missions. I hope it works. I try to keep my cool but they make it real difficult for me.

The enemy is shooting from the beach with heavy cannon fire at me. It is making 100-foot waterspouts. My private air force had to leave, low on fuel, so I have no protection at the moment. They will send a chopper to pick me up. I hope it is real soon.

I hit the water all right but immediately got tangled in my parachute. That 35-knot wind didn't help. It was dragging me under water as the chute sped toward the beach. I had to cut myself free with my knife. Damn enemy artillery moved closer. I climbed in my raft and they are firing at it. Those big waterspouts make me nervous. They have the right range, but they are about 100 yards off to their right.

Thank God, I can see two Marine choppers on the horizon. The enemy stopped firing since they spotted the choppers, too and want to throw everything at us when the choppers hover to pick me up. I plan to outsmart them. My old training in Naval gunfire spotting, tells me if I give them something to fire on, they will correct to the opposite side and start bracketing so I drop a smoke flare into the water next to my raft and let them shoot at it while I dive into the water and swim to where they were previously shooting. They will correct from there so that should be a safe place, except for the sharks, that is. If I am right, they will bracket in on the smoke because they think that is where the choppers will pick me up.

Lord I know I haven't been good about praying but as only you know, I only prayed for others, never for myself. Well, I felt your presence in the plane and you or someone told me to go for it to the gulf. Also when to eject. They have been shooting at me for thirty-five minutes now and either they are bad shots or you haven't let them get lucky. Now I need a little more help to get out of this mess. I sure would appreciate any help you would care to give. Well, that's all I have to say. Amen

The sharks didn't eat me and one of the Marine choppers swooped me out of the water with a horse collar. What a great feeling to be lifted safely into the chopper. The enemy saw the rescue and quickly changed their fire pattern but they were too late and the choppers flew rapidly out of range. Their shells exploded behind us. Here we are landing on the USS Princeton, a Marine Helicopter Carrier.

After a hot shower, I convinced the CO of a Helicopter Squadron to fly me to land. He flew me to an Army base where I hitched a ride in a Carabu back to Chu Lai, my home base. We landed in a driving rainstorm and almost crashed due to the strong winds and a downdraft short of the runway. It seemed like an appropriate way to end this day.

My good buddy, Pete Booher picked me up at the flight line with a jeep and took me to our makeshift officers club where I found a row of martinis waiting for me. They were Bombay Gin martinis, my favorite. I got a good night's sleep. A few days later, I was back up in North Vietnam, flying missions.

All that is written in my flight log on July 21, 1966 is the following:

Crashed, shot down, Tally Ho

SOME LIGHTER STUFF

THEY DESERVED TO LIVE

The letters on the tails of our A-4 attack jets were WK or in military jargon "whiskey kilo." My good buddy, Ed was flying on my wing as we returned to Chu Lai from a not very exciting support flight. Some of our Marines landed on a beach in South Vietnam and we flew over them to provide combat air support, in case they needed it. They didn't need us and we were returning with each of us carrying plenty of armament, including two 20mm cannons with full ammo and twelve 250-pound snake-eye bombs each. These bombs were fin retarded, so when you dropped them, a fin opened up to slow the bombs down. These bombs could be dropped at a very low altitude because the fins allowed the aircraft to fly ahead of them without any danger from the bomb blast. I contacted an Air Force forward air controller to see if he had any action for us. He gave me one of my most unique combat missions.

Ed was one of my best friends. We flew a lot together in all kinds of weather and in all kinds of combat conditions, but this one gave us many laughs over many martinis in O'Clubs for many years.

"Whiskey Kilo One, I have two VC hiding behind a tree," the forward air controller said.

"C'mon Kilo Two, this I gotta see." I said.

We are now entering the target area, a big hill that rises above the jungle and I have the air controller in sight. The top part of the hill is completely bare about 150 yards in all directions except for one large tree at the very top. Hiding behind this tree are two VC dressed in their traditional black pajamas, armed with grenades but don't have rifles. They can't leave because the air controller is flying tight circles around them and he holds them at bay with his pistol. As he circles, they circle behind the tree. It's a standoff. Oh well, this is an overkill considering the type and amount of ammo we carry for just two VC, but they are the enemy so let's go get them.

"Okay, Kilo Two, take a 10 second interval on me and we will each drop two bombs on this run.

"I'm rockin' in now."

Got the target in my bombsite. Bombs away. Hit just short of the tree. Hell, the concussion should knock them out.

"You get em, Kilo Two."

"Your bombs away." Hmmm, would you believe those guys are still there?

"Okay, this time I will run in from South to North and you run in from East to West. Drop two again."

Here we go, you little punks you are about to meet your maker.

I can't believe this. They are still there. We hit within a few feet of the tree and they are kind of shook up but they are still there. This is getting embarrassing. I notice that the air controller had nothing to say. Professional courtesy, I guess.

"All right, Kilo Two, let's strafe them. I will run in toward the East and you run in toward the West. Take a double interval on me so we don't fire at each other or run into each other."

Here we go. Full power, guns blazing, hitting the tree and all around it and dropping two more bombs now and pull out hard left to avoid hitting Kilo Two. He made his run.

No way! They are still there and that damn tree is still standing.

"Kilo two, join up tight on my right wing." Here we are, slowing down, lowering our landing gear, full flaps and opening the speed brakes. Down to landing speed now and approaching the tree.

We are flying right by the tree now and only about ten feet in the air. They are peeking at us from behind the tree. We can see each other very clearly.

I give them a hand salute. They salute back.

"Let's go home, Kilo Two, they deserve to live."

THE BLACK SHEEP

I can't remember the exact date but that isn't really important. I just returned from a night "TPQ" flight over North Vietnam. I never knew what TPQ stood for and still don't, but we flew a single aircraft every half hour over North Vietnam all night long every night. Radar units on the ground guided us to a point over the target area and we dropped our bombs on their command to harass the enemy more than anything else.

I returned from the refueling pits when I got the word "he" was here. I got rid of my flight gear and walked over to our makeshift Officer's Club. There he was at the bar surrounded by eight or ten pilots. Having just returned from a mission, I got first priority for the next drink at the bar. I grabbed a bar stool and placed it right next to him. I asked him if I could buy him a drink.

" I'll buy you one," he said.

For a fleeting moment, I felt like Clint Eastwood or John Wayne in some western cowboy flick. I bought him the next one and then we rolled the dice for them. I forgot what he drank but I had my usual Bombay gin martinis with a twist and waved the vermouth cork at it.

I really enjoyed meeting him and tried to out drink him. The Marine Corps sent him to Vietnam as a public relations thing and to help boost our morale. He was a Retired Marine General now. In his day he was the best and awarded the Congressional Medal of Honor, our Country's highest award. He was the Marine Corps highest ace, having shot down 29 enemy planes over the South Pacific during WWII. He commanded the famed Black Sheep Squadron, which was actually Marine Fighter Attack Squadron 214.

He wrote a best seller titled, "Bah Bah Black Sheep" and there were two television series about him and his Squadron. One was called "Black Sheep Squadron" and the other "Bah Bah Black Sheep." They both featured Robert Conrad as the star.

I found out in short order, I couldn't out drink him. Even though I was pretty good, I doubt if I could have out flown him in his prime either.

I had two Aviation heroes. One was Chuck Yeager and the other was this man.

His name was Gregory "Pappy" Boyington.

COMBAT NURSES

Hospital Ship

Each morning at Chu Lai, the white Hospital Ship with the large Red Cross silhouetted the sunrise over Chu Lai Bay where she anchored. At night the lights glistened from the ship across the Bay like an all-night party. The ship was anything but a party. Lives of wounded soldiers and Marines were saved there around the clock. We respected the medical staff of doctors, nurses, Corpsmen and all the Ship's Company that kept the Hospital Ship functioning.

Neil Levin

We sat on the beach and wondered what it was like on the ship. We wondered if the Nurses were pretty. You wonder things like that when you go months without seeing a woman.

We heard through the grapevine a Marine Helicopter Squadron from China Beach, outside of Danang, invited the doctors and nurses to a party at their base. They flew a couple helicopters out to the ship, picked them up, took them to the party and flew back to the ship a few hours later.

Those damn chopper pilots get everything. Hell, if they can do it so can we.

A few officers and I decided to invite a few doctors and nurses to a party in our Officer's Club on the Beach. We got the okay from the Group Commander and he sent the invitation.

He received regrets because the ship's boats couldn't land at our beach and we had no boats or helicopters.

We really wanted to see Nurses, so we built a small dock with help from the Engineer Battalion.

The party was on again. We offered food, booze, music, dancing and a good time.

The doctors and nurses came in two boats, about ten of each. I went down to our little dock to greet them and show them the way across the beach to our O'Club.

As soon as they docked, three doctors ran off the dock with pistols raised. They and the nurses were dressed in combat fatigues, but that was as close as they came to know how to act in a combat zone.

140

"Hold it," I yelled.

"The best way to get shot at here is to draw weapons and run."

"We walk everywhere and let our presence be known at all times."

"There are sentries behind trees and machine gunners man numerous foxholes on the beach."

"Follow me and we will all have a good time."

Much to our delight, the nurses were more beautiful than the doctors were stupid. We introduced each other, about forty of our officers and twenty of them. We had plenty of food and the booze flowed freely. We laughed and swapped stories and danced. It was a fantastic feeling to hold a woman in my arms on the dance floor. There was a lot of cutting in. Soon a doctor and a nurse took a walk on the beach, even though they were advised it wasn't safe. Then one after another the same combination disappeared, until only one nurse remained in a liplock with one of our pilots.

What the Hell is going on? I wondered. I went out on the beach and found a sentry standing guard. Looking down the beach, I noticed other sentries were standing, instead of in their foxholes out of sight.

"Marine, why aren't you and the other sentries in your fox holes? I asked.

"Sir, the fox holes are filled with doctors and nurses. What should we do about it?"

"Keep your eyes on the beach. They deserve a little slack."

It seems those doctors weren't stupid after all.

WHAT WOULD YOU DO?

FLIGHT LOG 24 OCT 1965-HOT PAD

On 24 October 1965, I flew a combat mission in South Vietnam, leading a flight of two A-4 attack jets. We were each armed with four 500-pound napalm tanks and 400 rounds of 20mm cannon fire. What should have been a routine combat attack mission turned out to be anything but.

I ask, "What would you do?"

We sit in our aircraft on the apron just off the end and to the side of the runway at Marine Corps Expeditionary Airfield, Chu Lai, commonly known as the "Hot Pad." We are at the "ready," which means we have troops in imminent danger and we are on a stand-by to launch quickly and come to their aid within minutes.

We get the signal from the Marine monitoring the hot line from the airfield tower to launch. We motion to our wingman we are ready and get a thumbs up from him. We both start our engines immediately and close our canopies. Our aircraft, already pre-flighted, and run through the preliminary checks prior to take-off, so we tell the tower we're scrambling on an Air Alert mission and taxi onto the runway ready for take-off.

We are in position for take-off and arm our "jet assisted take-off bottles," JATO bottles, for extra power since CHU LAI's runway is only 4,000 feet long. Our wingman waits until we are airborne before he commences his take-off run.

"Are you ready?"

"Good! Let's go."

Okay, full power from our engine and are at the 700-foot marker so let's fire our JATO bottles for the extra boost on take-off.

Wow, what a kick in the pants. Uh oh, we have a problem.

The bottle on our left side fired and then fell off of the airplane, meaning we have full power from the right side and no extra power from the left side. We have an asymmetrical take-off and the aircraft wanted to run off of the left side of this narrow runway. We have the following options:

Continue our take-off roll and use full right rudder to compensate for the left drift and try to get airborne with the additional power from only one JATO bottle with only 3,000 feet of runway remaining. Or we immediately throttle back to idle and drop our tail hook and catch the emergency cable at the end of the runway positioned there for take-off aborts. I calculated if we lost a JATO bottle and our gross weight at 18,500 pounds we could just barely get airborne by using all but a few feet of the runway, which would leave us no room for error.

"What would you do?"

If you chose to abort the take-off and catch the cable you chose correctly as far as safety is concerned, however we go for it because we are on an emergency mission and I know from experience I can get the aircraft airborne. If we run out of runway we can pull an emergency t-handle and jettison the four napalm tanks and pop this thing into the air since we will be 2,000 pounds lighter. The napalm tanks haven't been armed so they should not explode. If they do, they won't endanger any personnel since they will be past the end of the runway and in a clear area.

Almost up to take-off speed and here comes the end of the runway. Let's ease this stick back and see if we can fly.

Well, we just made it. We pick up speed and head for the target area. The forward air controller contacted us and briefed us on the target. There are about a dozen Marines pinned downed in a lightly wooded area, surrounded by open fields and about 30 of the VC fire at will from an open trench. You feel a little skittish at first but change your mind when you see all the tracer bullets zinging by our heads as we make our straight in run at them. For each tracer bullet that you see, there are four that you don't see.

I have the target in sight. Let's arm the napalm tanks and our cannons and go get the bad guys. We kiss off from our wingman and he followed us into the target as briefed.

We dive down to 50 feet above the ground and pick up max speed. Now run straight at them. They watched us come into the area and shoot at us with everything they have. This is when war gets real personal.

Here come the tracers right at us. Let's give them some fire back. I am firing both 20 mm cannons at them as we approach the target. I hope you feel better about this when your choice is either them or us. This is combat and it isn't nice.

Okay, drop the napalm tanks right in the trench.

"What was that?" Our right wing just took a sudden dip and we almost hit the ground and the aircraft is vibrating like a Mixmaster. Climb, climb and get altitude in case we need to eject. We head toward our base and climb to 5000 feet. I told our wingman to join up on us as soon as he comes off of the target and look us over. He reported the target was completely destroyed. I found out by slowing down the aircraft doesn't shake as much so we keep it slow and continue heading home.

Our wingman confirmed my worst fears. One of our napalm tanks under our right wing hung up and is armed. This in itself wouldn't be too bad because we could normally jettison it or land with it and get it disarmed. The tank hangs on a pylon under our wing and held in place by two lugs, one forward and one aft above the tank. Our predicament is the aft lug released and the tank is hung precariously by the forward lug and the lug is open. The live napalm tank banged wildly under our wing and caused the vibrations. That tank could explode at any moment.

Believe me the manual on ordnance safety doesn't handle this one.

We made it back to Chu Lai and orbit over Chu Lai Bay at 5,000 feet. We asked for advice from the so-called experts. The Base Ordnance Officer wanted us to fly to DANANG, 60 miles away and land on their 10,000-foot runway. I have done all I can do to get rid of this tank, including yawing the aircraft from side to side hoping the tank would slip off of the open lug and pulled straight up into a hammerhead stall where we let the airspeed go down to zero and we start falling down backwards. The damn tank won't shake loose. My nerves tensed because it looked like the probability it will fall off of the airplane when we land and burn since we have no way of disarming it in the air.

I talked to our Commanding Officer, Colonel Tom Mulvihill personally over the radio.

"Set up ideal conditions over the bay, head the airplane out toward the South China Sea and eject," he suggests.

"I will order a chopper pick you up in minutes. I don't care about the airplane. I want you back alive. Since you are on the spot, the decision is strictly yours."

That is why he is such a great leader and why he has been my mentor for years.

So, here are our options:

We land at DANANG as the Ordnance Officer wanted us to do, or we eject over the bay, or we land here at CHU LAI and catch a cable with our tail hook just like aboard an aircraft carrier.

If we land at DANANG and the tank comes off upon landing and burns, we could be engulfed in flames and burn down a 10,000-foot runway. We would have to eject on the runway and that could be pretty hairy. If you elected to eject over the bay, then you again made the sensible and safest decision.

However, I think we can save this airplane and our skin at the same time with a little luck. Do you feel lucky?

I decided to burn our fuel down to just enough to make one try for the cable on the CHU LAI runway, located at the landing spot as opposed to the abort cable at the end of the runway. I figured by the cable rapidly stopping us, it would throw the tank in front of us and burn away from us down the runway where the fire crew could put it out.

I requested the fire crew take position to the right side of the cable and slightly behind it. I also requested a helicopter hover close by and on my left side. I would open the canopy just before landing and the air-stream should break it off. When we land, if there is any fire, we will come out of the cockpit on the left side and have the chopper blow the fire to the right and away from us.

"Ready?"

Coming straight in for the landing. Lord, I hope this works. You could cut the tension with a cheese knife.

The Ordnance Officer is on the air.

"I want to go on record that I disapprove of this landing," he said.

Great, just what I need right now, somebody trying to cover his ass.

"Shut up and get off the air," I shouted.

We are lined up and flying steady and should touch down just before the cable. There, we landed and caught the cable. The plane stopped abruptly and the tank thrust forward, slammed into the runway just ahead of us. Luckily, the fuse bent upward instead of inward into the firing pin and rendered itself a dud and rolled down the runway.

"Thank you God, good to have you along."

Let's taxi this thing into the flight line and go get a cool one.

CHU LAI WATCH REPAIR

It was another of those warm muggy evenings in Chu Lai, in early 1966. Most nights were warm and muggy but changed to warm and wet during the torrential downpours that lasted for days on end. Everything felt wet.

All the days ran together and you did your best to get through until your tour was over and you went back home.

Some of us finished our flying for the day and didn't happen to be on the night flight schedule. We went to our makeshift officer's club earlier until it closed for the night. It was our way of unwinding after the day's activities and helped us pass the time.

The club closed and a few of us decided to trudge through the mud over to Lieutenant Colonel Tom Mulvihill's tent. His tent was one of the few places you could get good scotch or

Bombay gin. He and I both drank Bombay martinis with a twist of lemon peel and a wave of the vermouth cork. He introduced me to those damned things and I drank them for years. We liked to hang around him because he was one hell of a Marine and he made us feel welcome. He was fearless and put himself in the same harms way we experienced. He flew dangerous newly assigned missions first and we followed. The mark of a good leader.

Several of us sat at a table in the center of the tent having drinks. We told a lot of stories and laughed mostly at ourselves.

Major Dick Hawes, our Squadron Executive Officer sat in the corner playing chess and intimidating the hell out of his opponent. Dick was good at that, a fierce competitor whether in the air on a combat mission or on the ground playing chess or golf. A no-nonsense, straight forward Marine Officer later promoted to Full Colonel.

Major Jerry Hagen, a very impulsive type, terrific pilot and quick to act got into a fracus with the Air Group Executive Officer, both sitting at the end of the table. When Jerry had enough of him, he physically picked him up and threw him out of the tent into the rain and mud. Jerry turned and looked at Mulvihill.

"Serves him right," Mulvihill said, a man of few words.

Jerry was later promoted to Brigadier General.

It was getting late and we all had too much to drink.

Major George Ward sat next to him. George, a tall good looking Marine Officer completely dedicated to the Corps and his family, recently arrived from MCAS Iwakuni, Japan where he was assigned to the Air Wing staff. He wanted to fly combat missions so much he caught rides on the regularly scheduled cargo planes from Iwakuni before he got transferred to Chu Lai. He arrived on Friday evenings in Danang and hitched rides to Chu Lai anyway he could, by airplane or helicopter then flew combat missions with one of the squadrons on Saturday. He flew back to Iwakuni on Sundays.

"What time is it?" Mulvihill asked.

"Well it is ... Oh, my watch stopped again," Ward answered.

"Cheap watch."

"No it isn't."

"Cheap watch."

"No it isn't. It was an anniversary gift from my wife."

"Give it to me. I'll fix it."

"What can you do?"

"Give me the cheap watch. I'll fix it."

"Well, uh I guess." He handed him the watch.

Mulvihill placed the watch on the table and reached behind him for something. He grabbed a hammer and with one mighty blow smashed the anniversary gift into a million pieces.

AN ANGEL RODE MY WING

Everyone in the tent was stunned, eyes widened in disbelief, but George Ward was the first to speak.

"Why did you do that?" Ward bellowed.

"Cheap watch." Indeed a man of few words.

Unfortunately, Ward was later killed by enemy ground fire while flying a combat mission.

WEIRD STUFF

April 1966, I led a flight of two A-4 Skyhawk attack jets and stopped to refuel in Danang, then took off for our home base at Chu Lai.

Suddenly, I heard an emergency radio call on guard channel from an Air Force forward air controller that all military aviators constantly monitor. The forward air controller flew a small, light spotter plane.

"Any aircraft within fifty miles south of Danang, I have an emergency mission, please respond. Over," he said.

"Spotter One, this is Whisky Kilo, six, twenty miles south of Danang, 20,000 feet, armed with eight rocket pods, each carrying nineteen rockets and eight hundred rounds of 20 mike mike cannon fire. What is the nature of the emergency? Over," I replied.

"Helicopters can't get into an area to medivac wounded Marines due to extremely heavy anti-aircraft fire."

"Roger that. We are on top of an overcast, will penetrate it and be on our way."

I signal to my wingman to join up tight on my right wing and we punch down through the clouds, heading out to sea since there are no ground electronic navigating sites to fix our position. Penetrating inland toward the target could lead us into an unseen mountain since we fly blind in the clouds, using our cockpit instruments to establish true direction, airspeed, rate of descent, altitude and wing position.

"I'll call shortly under the overcast and crossing the beach feet dry," I said. "Give us headings to the target area at that time."

"Roger that."

We could contact radar control in Danang for assistance but this is an emergency and time is of the essence.

We broke into the clear under the overcast and we reverse our course to head in toward the coast and take heading directions from the forward air controller into the target area.

"Spotter One, we broke out in the clear at 1,200 feet, heading toward the beach."

"The target is three anti-aircraft guns situated at the points of a triangle, fifty yards apart in a wooded area and camouflaged. You have three separate targets."

Damned low cloud cover forced us to make low angle and altitude rocket runs at the targets and we were silhouetted against the cloud background like a shooting gallery and we are the ducks.

"Okay Kilo two, take a twenty-second interval on me and get in as close as you can before firing your rockets."

I turn toward the target, 100 percent power, rocket pods armed and set for salvo, to fire all nineteen rockets in the pod at once. We each have four pods so we make at least three runs to destroy all three enemy gun positions. The Marines marked the area with a white phosphorous mortar round.

I'm on the target and I have no trouble spotting them because all three anti-aircraft guns fire straight at me. Hundreds of tracer rounds whiz by me. I don't like this at all. I blaze away with my two 20mm cannons straight at them but it didn't slow them down.

"Wow, this is bad. I've been lucky so far because they lead me a little too much and miss my nose. When I pull up out of my dive after I fire the rockets, I pull up right into their gunfire. I don't see how I can avoid getting hit.

"This is it! This is when and where I die!"

Rockets are fired. You bastards are going to die with me.

Okay, this is it. Pull up.

What the hell is going on?

AN ANGEL RODE MY WING

I seem to be outside of the airplane and watch that nut in the cockpit, me, fly it through the enemy tracers.

All action slowed to a crawl. I felt really weird while the plane flew through that mess and didn't take a hit.

I am back in the cockpit and all is normal.

I saw one gun splatter.

I noticed my wingman fired way short of the two remaining guns.

Okay, bite the bullet and go after them.

I dove toward the targets and blasted the shit out of them, but this time stayed in the aircraft during my dives.

* * *

I served my combat tour in Vietnam and was stationed at MCAS Cherry Point, NC. I had this often-recurring dream and found myself in a room, one quarter of a Quonset hut in Danang. I knew it was my room. It had a cot with a red cover in the right-hand rear corner of the room, a locker, a refrigerator, a night table, a lamp and a small desk. I always felt relieved when I woke up and found myself nice and safe in my bed in Cherry Point.

I couldn't understand it since I had never been to any area of Danang, except the flight line or ever saw the inside of a Quonset hut there. I never saw a picture either.

I had this same dream for three years.

Neil Levin

In December of 1970, I was ordered back to Vietnam for a second tour of duty. On the morning of December 7th, I had the same dream, except I woke up to the real thing and the room was exactly as I pictured it for three years down to the red cover on the cot. I actually believe I had "out of body" experiences during those dreams and visited that room.

* * *

On a flight of two Skyhawks back to Chu Lai at three thousand feet and ten miles out, I'm ready to check in at point alpha and descend into the Chu Lai traffic pattern.

Looks like we have company. What the hell is he? I never saw anything like this before and he is a couple of hundred yards away extremely bright and shiny and oval shaped.

I turn toward him and he turns away. I turn away from him and he followed me. I get back on course and he gets back on course with me. He is toying with me. There he goes! In a split second he flew completely out of sight.

As my wingman and I walked in from the refueling pits, " Did you see what I saw?" I asked.

"Yes, and thank God you saw it too."

"Well, at least I know I'm not nuts."

We encountered a UFO.

THE DISTINGUISHED
FLYING CROSS

On December 6,1965. Captain Pete Booher, and I flew a bombing mission over Laos with two A4 attack jets. The target was a North Vietnamese arsenal with twenty-three buildings filled with firearms, ammunition and equipment to supply the Viet Cong, located on the famed Ho Chi Min trail. We destroyed the target completely and were both awarded the Distinguished Flying Cross.

Neil, left – Pete, second from left

Neil Levin

The CITATION reads as follows:

"For heroism and extraordinary achievement in aerial flight while serving with MARINE Attack Squadron 224 in action against insurgent communist (Viet Cong) forces in the Republic of Vietnam. On 6 Dec.1965. Major Levin was serving as Flight Leader of a two aircraft special mission to destroy a Viet Cong barracks and supply area. Although forewarned that unfavorable weather had forced all previous flights to divert to alternate targets, Major Levin and his fellow pilot exhibited resolute determination to complete the vital assignment. Judiciously climbing to conserve fuel, the two circled the target area for nearly forty-five minutes until a small break in the clouds unveiled the objective, which was situated about one hundred fifty feet from the top of the mountain ridge. With calm judgment and exceptional airmanship, the pilots launched their attack, navigating through a treacherous narrow valley and at a high rate of speed, turning directly into the steep mountain to expend their loads of two hundred fifty pound bombs and 20-millimeter ammunition. With a minimum of fuel remaining, they left beneath them a blazing inferno, which destroyed 23 structures and initiated three secondary explosions. By his exceptional performance, he contributed to dealing a severe blow to enemy operations in the area. Major LEVIN's superior aeronautical skill, indomitable determination and dedication to duty were in keeping with the highest traditions of the United States Naval Service."

Receiving the medal

That is what the Citation says. Here is what really happened.

Pete found a hole in the clouds and took a look under it and came back up to get me.

"Okay Pete, good work on finding that hole."

"An Air Force spotter says that if we can get through the clouds with tops at 16,000 feet to underneath with a ceiling of 1,500 feet, we will find a valley with steep mountains on both sides. We can run at the target nestled against the side of the mountain at the end of the dead end valley."

In order to get all the buildings, we made six runs each and dropped two bombs each on every run.

"Since you've been down there, I will follow you down and you lead the first run. Good luck. Let's go down."

Diving through the hole, we see the valley. Boy, it is really narrow. We came underneath an overcast at 1,500 feet, max power and pick up max speed.

Retard Bombs

The retard bombs have a fin that opens and creates drag slowing the bombs down, letting us drop the bombs at a very low altitude, since the aircraft is faster than the bomb we escape the blast. I feel like this is in a bowling alley and with my 20 mm machine guns blasting, I'm the ball speeding down the lane except the pins at the end of the alley are anti-aircraft guns their tracers spitting back.

Keep flying on a steady course to hit the target.

Steady, steady. I send two bombs right at the target.

Pete already hit his target with two bombs while I fly through fire and smoke on the pull up.

Pull up with 4 g's to climb up this mountain and we are in the clouds again, visibility nil. Once we pass the vertical, fly past straight up in our arc, we fly away from the mountain and are safe until 16,000 feet. We made it to the top of the clouds and in the clear and are ready for our next run.

The target is spread out and demands six runs each to hit all of the buildings and hopefully, some secondary explosions occur when their own ammo explodes. We may have to fly through the secondary explosions. With a little luck, it will work.

There's Pete. Good, he made it too. "Ready Pete. That was fun so let's go do it again."

We are again on top and in the clear after we have made our final run at the target. We were lucky, we both made it.

"It's a blazing inferno," the Air Force pilot in his spotter plane at the mouth of the valley said over the radio. "I spotted numerous secondary explosions. Christ, I've never seen anything like it. I want to report this in Saigon. What are your names?"

I gave him our names.

"Okay, let's go home, Pete. We are going to be sucking fumes on the landing. We may have to tap into a tanker to refuel. It will be close."

"Roger that," Pete answered.

I was later told these were the first two DFCs awarded to Marine Corps A4 Skyhawk pilots in the Vietnam War. The other services had them as well as some Marine F4 Phantom pilots and Marine Corps helicopter pilots. I flew because I was there and it was my job. Pete felt the same way. Although Pete and I were each awarded the Distinguished Flying Cross for this mission, I flew six other missions that met all the criteria for a DFC, but since I already had this one, the Marine Awards Board gave my wingmen DFCs on all of those missions, but never awarded me another one. I thought that was unfair since I led all of those missions and was responsible for most of their success.

For example, even though I was shot down during a bombing mission in North Vietnam after single handedly destroying a heavily defended bridge critical to the enemy's supply lines, I was awarded a Purple Heart, but not another DFC.

In fact, in one case when the target was very heavily defended, my wingman was too frightened to fly even near the target. He fired his rockets hundreds of yards short of the target. I flew in close, destroyed the target by myself and he got a DFC for it. I never told anybody about that, but he knows. I did tell him I would never let him fly as my wingman again.

I understand why the Marine Corps is so tight about awarding the DFC. It is the sixth highest combat award we have. I kind of got involved in some inter-service rivalry. What happened was the Air Force spotter pilot who took our names wrote up a full report to Air Force Headquarters in Saigon. They awarded both Pete and me the Distinguished Service Medal, which is a higher combat award than the DFC.

This embarrassed the Marine Corps because they were going to award us another Air Medal for the mission. I already had eleven Air Medals.

I was called before the Air Group Commander who asked me a question from the Commanding General.

"Which award do you prefer, the Distinguished Flying Cross from the Marine Corps or the Distinguished Service Medal from the Air Force?" he asked.

I told him since I was a Marine Corps pilot I would be honored to accept the Distinguished Flying Cross from the Marine Corps.

JO-ANNE

MEETING - R AND R - MARRIAGE

I transferred to NAS Pensacola, Florida in late 1969 for a tour of duty as Officer-in-Charge of the Preflight Division of Naval Schools Command. Promoted to Lieutenant Colonel and being the Senior Marine, I was the "Mean Marine" I once dreaded when a preflight student.

There were about twenty Drill Instructors, Navy lieutenants, Marine captains and sergeants under my Command. They each looked like they belonged on a Wheaties box cover. A great bunch of hard working "Gung Ho" guys in terrific shape.

My wife, Mary Alice and I separated. She lived eighty miles away in Mobile, Alabama with our four children and I lived temporarily in the BOQ (Bachelor Officer Quarters) on the air base and slated to transfer back to Vietnam for a second combat tour of duty in a year and a half. We planned to divorce when I returned from Vietnam. It was hard on all of us, especially my children.

I first saw Jo-Anne in the BOQ parking lot. She drove a cute baby blue Volkswagon Bug. I noticed her as she stepped out of her car. What a knockout, I thought. She had beautiful blonde hair and not a strand out of place. She wore a Navy nurse's uniform and wore it well. She carried herself in a way that showed pride as a Naval Officer, a nurse and as a woman. She held her head high, fully aware of her surroundings. She wasn't close enough for any dialogue like "hi, how are you?" I wouldn't have the foggiest idea what to say anyway, having never perfected a pickup line as a kid. I certainly didn't have one after eighteen years of marriage.

Our eyes met. Actually, I stared at her, wishing I were twelve years younger.

She smiled a genuine smile, a hello smile like you get from a happy person who really means hello. I gave a half-hearted smile back.

Things went through my mind. Why haven't I seen her before? Is she just passing through or stationed here? Will I ever see her again? Anyone that beautiful must have either a husband or a boyfriend in her life. Hell, what am I thinking? I am a Senior Officer. She's a young Junior Officer and fraternization is frowned upon in the military. She must be about twenty-two years old and I am thirty-seven. What could she possibly see in me?

Our quarters were in separate buildings so we left in different directions. I turned and watched her leave the parking lot. She turned and briefly glanced to see if I was watching.

That did it. I had to see her again. I know I was attracted to her beauty, but it seemed more than that. I felt destined to meet her, like finding my soul mate.

The officers dined in the Officers Mess Hall close to the living quarters. Senior officers sat at a large straight table, while junior officers filled the rest of the dining hall. Navy nurses also sat at the senior table.

I had breakfast later than usual the next morning with my usual argument with the Navy officers about who are better fighter pilots, Navy or Marine. I claimed all they talk about was landing on aircraft carriers. Marines also land on aircraft carriers, and talked about something worthwhile to do between takeoff and landing.

I was in a joking but heated discussion with two Navy pilots when she came into the room and sat across the table from me. I felt excited and nervous at the same time. My God, here she is, my dream girl. Needless to say, I was delighted, surprised and in complete awe. She's even prettier close up, so fresh and alive. Her smile made me feel I was special to her, too.

Finally, my chance to meet her. I felt I had to say something clever but my best efforts could only produce a "Good morning."

"Good morning sir," she replied.

I didn't want her to call me sir but realized it was a proper response at a senior officers table.

I fantasized her calling me Neil and saying "Yes, I'll marry you."

We engaged in small talk. I learned she was from Raleigh, NC and her favorite song was "Raindrops Keep Falling On My Head."

"You have no Southern accent," I said.

"I decided it wasn't something I wanted to carry through life but I can turn it on when I want to."

She just finished her night shift at the hospital and needed sleep and I was late for work so we left.

Wow, she's not only beautiful and friendly, but intelligent, too.

I saw her many times over the next couple weeks, even driving by, she always waved. She went to "Happy Hour" at the O'Club on Friday nights with her girlfriend who was also her roommate. Again, she smiled and waved. If I wasn't so busy playing Mr. Macho, rolling the dice at the bar for martinis, I would have joined her.

One Thursday evening, the student class graduating Friday morning invited me to attend their pre-graduation beer party because the guest speaker for their graduation was a Marine General. Normally high-ranked Naval Officers were the Guest of Honor. He also presided over the graduation parade from the reviewing stand on the parade grounds. As the students Commanding Officer, I was in charge of the parade.

I attended the party and met the General.

"General, I remember when I attended my first parade after I arrived for duty, I relieved another Marine LtCol. He and I sat in the reviewing stand next to each other accompanied by about a dozen Navy officers. As the parade passed by, the marching band played the Marine Corps Hymn. Of course, we two Marines stood at attention. He said, 'Navy officers didn't even stand at attention for Anchors Away at that Command. I was too embarrassed to stand by myself so I am glad you are here today.' I asked him to attend the parade the following Friday and every officer in the stand would rise and stand as the Marine Corps Hymn played.

"When the parade ended I asked the Navy Chief who led the Marching Band to accompany me on the field. We paced and measured and placed a small flag at a designated spot on the field. I told him to always play the Marine Corps Hymn as he passed that flag. From that time on, each Friday as the Hymn played, all Officers in the reviewing stand stood at attention because at that precise moment our National Flag passed by. The Navy officers never caught on to my scheme. Mark one point for the Marines."

The General loved the story.

I had a couple of beers and left the party early because of steak night at the Officer's Mess and I didn't want be too late. I arrived around 7:30 PM to an almost empty mess hall.

I spotted Jo-Anne dining with one of the junior officers. With the senior table empty, I joined them and she introduced me to her friend, Allen, a male Navy nurse.

They just finished their dinner and Allen asked, "Jo-Anne, are you ready to leave?"

"No, I think I will stay here and talk to Neil for a while."

"I think you better leave with me."

"I'm staying," she said firmly.

He left.

Maybe she sees something in me too, I thought.

After dinner, I asked her to go to the Officers Club, have a few drinks and get to know each other better and she agreed. We changed to civilian clothes, met a half hour later and went to the club. She wore her long blonde hair down and she looked gorgeous.

We had a fun time talking and dancing and I felt a special chemistry between us.

After that evening, we saw each other on a frequent basis.

I rented a mobile home close by on Pensacola Bay where my kids could visit me on weekends. I missed them terribly and I was very sad about my personal life. Jo-Anne came by often and added a woman's touch, helping to make it more homelike.

It seemed she was the only bright star in my life.

Things worked out well. When she worked the night shift at the hospital and I couldn't see her, I went to the Pensacola Kennel Club, betting dog races. I gave most of my money to Mary Alice for the kids and only had about $250.00 a month to live on. I studied dog racing and covered my personal expenses by winning at the track.

We were very much in love and happy. As all good things eventually come to an end, I received orders transferring me back to Vietnam. I hated to leave her but I was a Marine and duty calls.

* * *

I arrived back "in Country" as we called Vietnam, in Danang on December 7, 1970. Hoping to command a Squadron, I landed the Marine Air Group-12 Logistic Officer's position, better known as Group S-4. Normally a boring job for a pilot, I was responsible for an embarkation plan to move the Air Group, including all men and equipment back to the States by air and ship. It kept me busy on the ground but I flew some combat missions at night.

I just settled in my new quarters, one quarter of a Quonset hut, when the damn enemy rocket attack started. I dove out of my cot and hit the deck face down, throwing my helmet on my head and my mattress on my back. I'm sure back in Hell, I thought.

During the attack, I focused on the two weeks Jo-Anne and I spent together in California, waiting for my flight assignment on an airliner to

Vietnam. We took in all the sights, starting with Disneyland and we had a wonderful time together.

Kaboom! That one hit close and shook the whole Quonset hut. Now I'm pissed off. The next morning, I learned the rocket attack was almost a nightly event.

Two weeks later, I inspected equipment in an open lot next to our supply depot. I heard a rifle shot zing by my head from a sniper. I dove behind a truck and grabbed my weapon, a .38 caliber pistol but couldn't see the sniper. I waited a while then left the area.

Now, I'm really pissed off. I'm shot at in the air, on the ground and rocketed at night.

Jo-Anne and I wrote every day and obvious by our letters, we were both hopelessly in love.

Six weeks later, I requested R and R and asked Jo-Anne to meet me in Hawaii. A Marine Captain joined our Air-group who was born and raised on Kauai. Being a pilot in the Hawaii Air National Guard, he transferred into the Marine Corps. He suggested Kauai for R and R and gave me some tips about where to go.

My airliner took off for Hawaii and I arrived on March 16, 1971. My God, what a psychological experience from combat in Vietnam to the serenity of Hawaii.

Jo-Anne arrived the day before me because of the uncertainty of our flight schedule. About fifty of us were taken into Honolulu on military busses and led to a staging area like a bunch of cattle and briefed about being nice while in civilization.

Jo-Anne arrived with a group of women who patiently waited for us. She wore a blue Hawaiian dress, her blonde hair flowing over her shoulders and my heart melted. I held her tightly and didn't want to let go.

We flew to Kauai and stayed in an upstairs bungalow on the oceanfront at Poipu Beach. Two doves flew to our porch railing and walked into our room. I wondered if the hotel management sent them. Everything was bamboo, palm trees, clear blue ocean and Hawaiian music. We had five wonderful days there, sightseeing and being together.

Most memorable to me was Hanalei Bay where the movie "South Pacific" was filmed. We dined in the restaurant overlooking the bay. Another event was a visit to the town of Nawiliwili for dinner. The friend who recommended Kauai suggested a combination pharmacy, bar and restaurant for the best Mai-Tai in Hawaii. When I mentioned his name to the pharmacist he led us to a table, then ordered two Mai Tais for us and insisted we have dinner and drinks on him. We had a wonderful evening. One by one, the shop owners of Nawiliwili showed up after closing their shops and we all had a fun party.

Sadly, on the sixth day we left Kauai and flew back to Honolulu International Airport. I waited with her until her plane left. Watching it disappear over the horizon, I wondered if I would ever see her again. One of the nice things about Kauai, nobody was trying to kill me. I had a couple hours until my plane left, plenty of time to reminisce about the past week and wonder about the future. I decided if I managed to stay alive, I wanted to marry her as soon as my divorce was final.

After a long grueling flight back to Vietnam, we finally landed at Danang late at night. I hitched a jeep ride to my little Quonset hut and soon slept soundly. At 2:00AM the rocket attack started. Seven rockets hit all over the air base, only one of them on the Marine side of the field. The Air Force side took numerous hits, one of them destroying a fuel tank.

Was that R and R a dream or did it actually happen? What an emotional swing.

* * *

I decided to propose to her as soon as I came home from the War. I needed a ring so I ordered a Marquise cut solitaire full carat diamond from Antwerp, Belgium out of a catalogue. It arrived after a few weeks and I hid it in my locker. Each time we had a rocket attack, I thought how pissed I would be if they destroyed that diamond. I wouldn't even send it to her. I wrapped it in a tissue and carried it in my pocket on the flight home.

I came home on June 10, 1971. After reporting for duty at Marine Corps Air Station El

Toro, California, I took leave immediately and flew to Pensacola. I proposed and gave her the diamond and only spent a couple days. She chose the ring setting later.

I wanted to see my kids in Mobile. I saw them the next day. I missed them so much and it broke my heart to leave them again, but I had no choice. My divorce wasn't going as planned and I needed to take charge of it in California.

I left my car in Pensacola when I went overseas so I drove it to California. Jo-Anne rode with me to El Paso and flew back to Pensacola.

Jo-Anne left active duty with the Navy Nurse Corps and went on active reserve status. She came to join me in California. Active reserve status meant working in a Naval Hospital one weekend a month and two weeks during the summer.

She earned a position as Head Nurse, Cardiac Care Unit in Mission Community Hospital in Mission Viejo, California where she worked on a full time basis.

We married in a little chapel on the air base on May 20, 1972. It was a military wedding with an arch of crossed swords and all that good stuff. We had a wonderful reception in the Officers Club attended by many of my Marine buddies and her nurse friends.

I commanded a squadron at El Toro so Jo-Anne was the CO's wife and a damn good one. The officer's wives in our squadron had a lot of respect for her, even though many of them were older than she. As an officer herself, she knew how to command respect. I was very proud of her.

I retired from the Marine Corps in 1973. Jo-Anne stayed in the Navy Reserve. She returned to active duty during the Gulf War for a year and retired recently with the rank of Navy Captain.

We divorced after eight and a half years and both since remarried. I don't think either of us knew exactly why we divorced because we were so very much in love, but we just grew apart. We remain close friends over the years. She influenced my life and my Marine career in a very positive way and I am grateful for her in my life. We formed a bond that remains today.

We came a long way since I saw her step out of that Volkswagon.

THE POST WAR YEARS
AND RETIREMENT

      I returned to the States from my second tour of duty in Vietnam on the 10th of June, 1971. After the airliner took off from Danang, I breathed a sigh of relief and for the first time in many months. I felt safe. Most of the excitement was left behind and the remaining couple of years were rather quiet, but not insignificant. I commanded H&MS, a Headquarters and Maintenance Squadron at MCAS El Toro, California. It handled the administrative needs of the Air Group Staff Officers and men, plus the maintenance needs of the Air Group Aircraft that were not handled by the individual Squadrons. The Squadron had over 500 men in it. The Squadron Command was challenging, and it went well, but my flying days seemed rather humdrum. I flew a few A4 Skyhawks, but mostly as co-pilot in C-117 Transport planes. We dropped Marine paratroopers over Camp Pendleton or we took Marines to places like The Air Force Academy in Colorado for inter-service pistol and rifle competition. Occasionally, we transported troops to and from MCAS Yuma, Arizona.

We flew the C-117s to Miramar and North Island and picked up or dropped off the personnel from San Clemente Island.

The Navy practiced land carrier landings at an airfield on the island, 75 miles west of San Diego out in the Pacific Ocean and kept a contingent of men stationed there to handle the operations of the airfield. Isolated there for six months at a time, they welcomed a chance to get off the island for a few days every once in a while. As a perk the men caught lobsters within legal limits and sold some of them to us. It was nice coming home to El Toro with fresh lobsters for dinner. After a year and a half as CO of the Squadron, I turned the Colors over to another Marine LtCol.

I spent the remaining few months at El Toro as the assistant intelligence officer of the Air Wing and found this interesting because we were very personally involved with the return of our Prisoners of War from Hanoi. I felt good that I took part in the planning for their return.

I retired from the Marine Corps on the 30th of April 1973. We had a parade to honor us retirees that day and I felt very sad when it was over. I realized I would never wear the uniform of my beloved Marines again. I drove home alone and as I approached the main gate I suddenly got an idea.

Neil Levin

The Marine sentry at the gate gave me a snappy salute as Marine sentries always do. I returned his salute with my own and then did a strange thing.

I stopped the car, got out and approached the Marine.

"Your salute is my last in uniform," I said, handed him a one-dollar bill and explained, "When I got my first salute as a newly commissioned officer twenty years earlier from my drill sergeant, I gave him a one-dollar bill, as was the custom. And I want to give you a dollar for my last salute."

He beamed with pride and said "Thank you, sir."

I drove through the gate, holding back emotional tears.

Neil, 2001

I had a civilian commercial flying license and rented different airplanes from Newport Beach California at Orange County Airport or San Juan Capistrano, California before they closed their tiny strip. I flew mostly Cessna and Pipers of all makes and sizes and limited my flying to the local area. I decided to settle down in Southern California during my retirement. I landed in interesting places like Big Bear Lake Airport in the mountains and a little strip 100 miles out on the Southern California Desert called Desert Center.

I bought into an aircraft partnership with two friends. We bought an eighteen-year-old, four-seated Piper Cherokee 140 for $10,000 and spent another $5,000 fixing it up. It was a fun airplane. The most fun I had in it was flying out to Santa Catalina Island and landing on their small runway on top of the mountain. It's a 1610-foot drop to the ocean down sheer cliffs at both ends of the runway. I took friends over to their "Restaurant in the Sky" and ate Buffalo burgers then flew the twenty-six miles back to Orange County Airport.

When I retired from the Marine Corps, I vowed I would never work for anyone but myself. I had a tough time making the transition from the structured life of a Career Marine to life in a freewheeling and dealing civilian society where it seemed nobody was in charge. I guess I did okay as an entrepreneur though, because I never worked for anyone else.

I still miss flying in the Marine Corps and that wonderful feeling of power and speed. I never felt I was riding in a jet airplane, more like I strapped it on and went flying as if the airplane was a part of me and I was the one flying.

On the way to Catalina

THE WALL

In May of 1996, I visited the Vietnam War Memorial Wall in Washington, DC for the first time. I saw it on television, in newspapers and magazines many times and never had any strong feelings about it. I always thought it was a good thing since it would remind people in the future, men and women gave their lives in this war, too, and should be honored and remembered just as much as those who died in other wars.

I never thought, "Well, it's about time" like many other Vietnam Veterans and I never complained about the lack of enthusiasm for us when we returned from Vietnam. I went on with my life and except for dreams of combat that all but disappeared since I started writing about them, I don't think about it much.

Walking down a path, I approached the Wall and was amazed at the number of people there. I estimated one hundred or more. I was pleased there was no graffiti, no protesters like the ones at the White House and the Wall was in perfect condition. The mood was somber. As I neared the Wall, I felt myself fill with emotion. I felt sad. I knew some of the names on the Wall but I really wasn't interested in finding them. I was aware there were 58,000 names on that Wall and all of them had families and friends and they each gave the ultimate sacrifice for their Country.

I walked to the center of the Wall and faced it and tried to hold back the tears, welling inside me. A young African American man approached me.

"Did you serve in Vietnam?" he asked.

"Yes, I did," I replied

"Thank you for going there and I am glad you made it back. May I shake your hand?"

All of a sudden I realized I waited twenty-five years for someone to do what he did. Shake my hand and say thanks for going. I told him so and I thanked him, telling him it was a nice thing he had done for me.

He walked away.

Then I cried.

LAURIE

After Jo-Anne and I divorced and romance during my retirement years was like a yo-yo, up and down. I fell in and out of love, had relationships, three engagements and even a short three and a half year marriage more like a long date that didn't work out.

Then I met Laurie on a blind date set-up by a mutual friend. I wasn't wild about blind dates since my college days when our Fraternity from Philadelphia went to a Ball hosted by a brother Fraternity in another city.

We all congregated around a drug store and picked cards with our dates names and phone numbers out of a bowl. I immediately went to a phone booth and called the number.

"Hello," she said in a deep smooth sexy voice.

"Hi, I'm Neil and I'm calling about the Ball tonight," I said.

"Oh fine. I'm looking forward to it."

"You sure have a sweet voice and you sound very pretty."

"Thank you, but I'm really not very pretty."

"C'mon, you're just saying that. I'll pick you up at seven-thirty if that's okay"

"Seven-thirty will be fine. See you then."

I arrived promptly at seven-thirty, rang her doorbell and she wasn't kidding. She looked a lot like George Washington. We went to the Ball and danced. I showed her a good time and tried my best to be a gentleman. She was very nice, but let's face it, when you are nineteen, looks are important. I felt very shallow but decided blind dates are not for me.

So after all these years, I'm faced with another blind date. My friend, Monte, who lived in the apartment below me thought Laurie and I would like each other and gave me her phone number. I tossed it on my coffee table and found it three weeks later when I cleaned the table.

What the hell, let's give it another try, I thought.

We talked on the phone and she sounded real pretty. Oh Christ, here I go again. When will I ever grow up. We made a dinner date.

I nervously rang her doorbell and hoped a George Washington or Abraham Lincoln look-alike didn't answer.

The door opened and there, framed in the doorway, stood a gorgeous blonde with a beautiful smile, a friendly air about her, stylishly dressed and she had class written all over her. Laurie is a California native and looks the part.

We went to dinner at the Marina and spent the evening trying to be ourselves and impress each other at the same time. We asked all the awkward questions normally asked on a first date. The answers were good enough for us to decide on a second date to "know more about you."

I figured she like me but when we reached her house my bubble burst while just inside the doorway she ushered me out and let the cat in.

I guess I didn't impress her that much.

I did the cool thing and waited a few days before I called her, but I didn't want to see anybody else. She did the cool thing by not waiting for my call and had three dates in the meantime.

Before I met Laurie, I discussed my dating situation with a friend, Gregory, a CPA and a "by-the-numbers" kind of guy. I complained I was dating frequently but they had no substance and I really wanted to have a serious long-range love interest. He suggested I list all the positive attributes I wanted and when I found the woman who had most of them she would be my woman. Sounds just like a CPA. I wrote a list and he put it in his desk drawer. I wrote nineteen items important to me at the time.

Laurie and I dated and I felt drawn to her and after a few dates, we talked about an exclusive relationship.

When she mentioned it to her friends they jokingly made remarks like "You mean you are

187

going with a Jewish guy?" — "That's not so bad but a former Marine. Do you think you can handle that?" — "But really Laurie, a Republican?"

I questioned my motives and asked Gregory what he thought. He pulled out the list and read each item. Laurie had all the qualities.

"So what are you waiting for?" he asked.

We had fun and laughed a lot and enjoyed each other and it all felt right.

"Wow"

AN ANGEL RODE MY WING

After six months, Laurie found herself between jobs and I just had my first granddaughter born in Alabama so I asked her to take a cross-country trip with me to visit my children in Alabama and my mother in Florida. She agreed and I planned a twenty two-day trip, driving the Southern route across Texas to Alabama and on to Florida and return with the last night visit with Laurie's cousins in Phoenix. I figured if we didn't kill each other driving across Texas, we had a good chance to be a long lasting couple.

We almost killed each other in Texas but we managed to work our way through our differences and we both saw that as a very positive step.

The trip went extremely well and we both realized we were in love. Driving north out of Tucson, I looked at her across the seat and realized I wanted to marry her and spend the rest of my life with her.

"You are one hell of a woman," I said.

She acknowledged she was.

We married on August 18, 1990 and it was one of the best things I have done in a long time. We have a wonderful marriage filled with all the right stuff. It took me four times to finally get it right. I couldn't ask for a more loyal, loving, beautiful partner. We are there for each other through thick and thin, like her recovery from cancer and mine from quadruple by-pass surgery. We have complete trust in each other with confidence this marriage is right for both of us.

189

She knows what she wants and she knows how to handle me. For example, we rented condos in Solana Beach for twelve years when she decided we needed to buy a home somewhere. I was dead set against it until I woke up one morning, living in our home in Oceanside, CA. I still can't figure what happened.

Thank God for her in my life.

And I was afraid of another blind date.

THE REUNION

On the 25th of September 1997, about 17 Marine Officers, members of VMA-224 during the Vietnam War, met each other for a Squadron reunion for the first in thirty-one years since we returned home from Vietnam in 1966. Most of the officers were pilots that flew with each other for a period of three years with the final thirteen months in combat flying out of Chu-Lai, South Vietnam. They flew A-4 Attack jets and the Squadron was known throughout the Marine Corps as "The Top Gun Squadron," indicative of the fine caliber of pilots that flew in this Squadron. "The Reunion," was held in New Bern, NC because it coincided with the Marine Corps Aviation Association Annual Convention and it put us only sixteen miles from MCAS Cherry Point, NC where we were originally stationed and trained for combat.

Back in the States, we scattered to the winds. Some of us stayed in the Corps until retirement, others completed one or two tours of duty then left the Corps for civilian life, and many still fly for the airlines, but a few have recently retired from the Airlines. Some kept in touch with each other but for the most part we went our separate ways and lost touch.

We trained hard for our combat tour back in the sixties. We flew hard, played hard and we knew what to expect from each other. When we went to Vietnam, we were ready to go. When we returned, there wasn't much in the way of celebration and most of us went on with our lives and had little to say about that particular time in our lives. We didn't feel we had to explain to anyone why we were there. We served our Country and served it well. This reunion was important to us because we all know what we went through together and haven't really shared it with others and didn't seem to have a need to talk about it so by being together even briefly, it felt good.

We were interested in finding out what each of us had been up to all these years and what we were doing now. Were we still married or divorced and married again or did we ever marry? Where we lived now, what do we do and so forth.

If the others felt as I did, then my Marine Corps career was a highlight in my life and the three years served in that particular Squadron was the highlight of my career.

As the airliner took off in a driving rainstorm, a squall that preceded hurricane Linda a couple of hundred miles South of San Diego, I felt a little nervous about this reunion. After all, thirty-one years is a long time and I was sure we all changed considerably. Would anyone even recognize me? Would I recognize them? I was glad to be going though and thankful for the few people who planned and organized the reunion. It wasn't easy finding everyone, coordinating everything and getting the information out. I appreciate those efforts and the people who made it all happen know who they are and so do those who attended. I purposely left names out of this because this isn't about individuals, but about us catching up with each other. Actually, those who couldn't attend are just as much a part of it as those who did.

My plane landed at New Bern in bad weather as well. I noticed the airport hadn't changed and still had a small one-room terminal. I had breakfast, a piece of ham and cheese on an English muffin out of a microwave oven at the snack bar. Hertz ran out of cars so they gave me a truck. I hope someone asks me if I got a nice car from Hertz so I can say "not exactly" like their recent television commercials.

After checking into my hotel room and changing, I headed over to the Sheraton Hotel where the Squadron had a hospitality suite on the fifth floor. I walked down the long hallway toward the VMA 224 Banner that hung over the door at the end. I felt exhilarated and excited. Laughter came from behind the open door and all of a sudden I felt part of it all again and thrilled to be there.

As soon as I entered the room I was recognized, which was a big relief to me. I had to do a double take at a couple of them but some of them hardly changed. Most of them were in their mid-twenties when I last saw them and now they were in their fifties. A few of us are now in our sixties and seventies. I felt the energy in that room and the excitement of friends once bonded finding each other again. We were a proud bunch and it still feels the same.

We visited MCAS Cherry Pt. the next day and also Morehead City the following day and spent delightful hours together, eating, drinking, laughing and remembering those that couldn't make it and those few that passed on. We honored our CO, who has since passed on, by presenting his wife with a framed picture of him.

I used to hang out with Pete Booher and Ed Loney, two pilots in the Squadron. We flew, drank and even played golf together. We used to tee off every Saturday morning at 0830 when we were stationed at Cherry Pt and since then one of our trio, Ed was killed. A highlight of the reunion for me was when Pete and I stood on the first tee at the golf course and just quietly paid our respects to Ed.

For years, I wondered what happened to those wonderful guys that made up the "Top Gun Squadron." I am not one to live in the past. I live in the now and for the future but this reunion was like reaching way back in my life and pulling a blanket up to cover me.

It felt warm.

WHAT EVER HAPPENED TO GEORGE?

I hadn't seen George for many years and for the better part of 47 years. I asked myself, "what ever happened to George?"

George is George Kretschman and I met him on the 6th of April, 1953, the day we both checked into the Naval Aviation Cadet Program at the Naval Air Station, Pensacola, Florida.

As Navcads, we faced a grueling preflight class before a year and a half of flight training. Our Class was 16-53 and a damn good class. George and I became good friends and roommates in preflight and we hung out a lot all the way through our basic training at Pensacola for a year until we both went to Advanced Training in Corpus Christi, Texas. We helped each other with our studies and our physical tests and our flying to get through the Program. We covered for each other and we even hung out together on our time off. We used to go out on an off-duty runway on

Sunday afternoons and fly the model airplanes George built. We went into town on Saturdays and tried to forget the Program although hard to do because we were required to wear our uniforms all the time during preflight. I could usually go after I finished marching off my time on the parade grounds as punishment for accumulative demerits. George had a mischievous look in his eyes, but he, a nice kid from New York, went right by the book, while I, a wise guy from New Jersey had an angle for everything and got caught quite often. After 50 demerits, they washed you out and I really pushed the envelope. George was a model cadet and if he ever got into trouble or nearly, it was usually my fault. I never could figure out why he wanted to be my friend. Whatever the reason, I was glad for the friendship.

He said he first laughed at me the day after our arrival for our traditional haircuts and watched when my long black curly locks hit the floor. We made fun of the Drill Sergeants and we laughed a lot. The program wasn't easy and about 25% of the cadets got washed out, but George and I, determined to get through it, supported each other and proudly made it and earned our Wings and became Commissioned Officers. He went to the Navy while I went into the Marine Corps. We went to different Air Bases and we lost touch after that. The last I heard, George was flying PBMs out of Trinidad.

I finally decided to do something about that nagging question and I located him on the computer. I almost gave up when I couldn't find him in New York and then I remembered how he always loved Florida and would like to retire there someday. I hit pay dirt and came up with about ten Kretschmans in Florida and George one of them. I called and got an answering machine. I didn't want to leave a message so I sent an e-mail to him and described myself and asked if he was the right George Kretschman. He quickly responded by e-mail and we got together on the phone. I learned he tried to find me too. Since I planned to visit my mother in Florida in April 2000, we decided to meet at that time.

Since George and his wife, Ethel would drive from the Western side of Florida and me from the Eastern Coast, we decided to meet in a town George picked, about a seventy-five mile drive for each of us.

Driving out past the West Palm Beach Airport and heading West, I felt the excitement of meeting my old friend again. After all, the major part of a lifetime had passed. He sent me a recent picture of himself and Ethel so I knew what they looked like today, but since he had no picture of me, I told him I would wear a ball cap with USMC on it. We weren't 21 anymore and certainly we changed a lot.

I drove into the beginning of the Florida Everglades and Clewiston was now only about 30 miles away. The land was as flat as Kansas. It was a perfect day about 78 degrees, not that the weather even mattered, but the sun was shining and there was a warm breeze.

I entered the town on the main street and passed the typical stuff, the hardware store, post office, farm equipment stores, feed stores, a car lot and the City Hall and a couple of cheap motels and a supermarket. I expected only a General store would be there and was surprised to see a small but bustling community. The town was Clewiston, Florida, and we met at the Clewiston Inn, which is the largest building and nicest in Clewiston. I think they built the building and then a town around it. They didn't have a restaurant in the inn, they had a dining room, and probably the classiest place in town too.

I was thrilled to see The Clewiston Inn at the far end of town. We were to meet at high noon and I felt a little like Gary Cooper because of the classic movie "High Noon." I was right on time and entered the lobby. I felt a rush of adrenaline. George and Ethel would come back into my life after a long time any minute now.

They walked in and looked great. We recognized each other immediately and embraced each other. We went into the dining room and had a two-hour lunch. I noticed George still had a mischievous look in his eye. Who would have thought 47 years ago, we would next meet in a tiny sugar town in the middle of Florida.

We talked about our past relationship and then attempted to bring each other up to date. We talked about our careers, his in air traffic control after he left the Navy. We talked about our kids and families.

After lunch, we left the hotel and walked to an adjoining park where we sat at a picnic table under a beautiful shade tree. Everything was so green and fresh and well watered. We spent another two and a half hours and solved all of the world's problems. It's interesting how much we had in common in our thinking, though our lives were quite different.

George and Neil, 2000

It was evident how we accepted each other unconditionally. George had a real stable life, a full career in air traffic control. He even survived the Reagan firing of so many air traffic controllers, years ago. I am especially proud of both George and Ethel for being married for 47 years and looking for that magical 50 years to come up. George had been the Exalted Ruler of the Elks Lodges in both Homestead and Deep Creek, Florida. He now lives in Port Charlotte, Florida where he is a Mason and he and Ethel are active in their Church. Like I said before, George always does things by the book.

I gave Ethel a box of See's candy from California and we said our good-byes after what George describes as a very short four and a half hours, where we really just touched the tip of the iceberg about our lives.

Our meeting was very special because we weren't just old friends, but special friends since our friendship occurred at a critical time in our lives, a time when we never knew what was in store for us the next day. A time when some of our friends died in flight training accidents, trying to do the same things we were called on to do. Although full of anxieties, we gave each other courage to go on, never doubting we would make it where so many failed.

We decided we would keep in touch from then on and meet when we could. I drove the 75 miles back to my mother's house and felt good. I felt inspired to write something about the wonderful experience that day on the 28th of April, 2000 when I had the answer to "What ever happened to George?"

MEMORIAL DAY, 2001

THEY ALL HAD NAMES

Memorial Day, 2001.

I ask myself, the question, "The memory of what? Is it the memory of actions, battles and deeds? No, it's the memory of people."

People who have died in the service to their Country, while defending our Constitution and abiding by the oath they took. None of these magnificent Warriors wanted to die for their Country, they were there doing their jobs.

As General George Patton once said, "The object of war is not to die for your Country, but to make the other bastard die for his."

These people have names. They are people I served with and some of them were my friends. I never shared these thoughts before with anyone, but I feel I want others to know about these people that make up my Memorial Day.

Six of my roommates were killed in plane crashes during my flight training as a Naval Aviation Cadet in Pensacola, Florida and four of them while practicing for aircraft carrier landings. I know I got pretty nervous while in training to land aboard the aircraft carrier USS Monterey, a straight-decked carrier. Word got out and nobody wanted to be my roommate.

* * *

His name was Willie Russmeisal, a nice guy. We were cadets together. He was an easy goin' laid-back guy with a Southwest drawl. We were friends and covered each other's backs. I always felt I could count on Willie in a pinch. I was secretly married and my wife at the time lived in a little one-room apartment in Corpus Christi while I was stationed forty-five miles away in Kingsville, Texas with Willie. With our hectic schedule of flight training, I seldom got to see her and a long weekend came up and as luck would have it, I was scheduled for an overnight deck watch. Willie had no plans so I asked him to take my watch and he agreed to do it for five dollars. Doesn't seem like much, except when you got paid $108.00 a month it went a long way. I went home Friday night and was rudely awakened by Willie knocking on my door early Saturday morning.

"You're in big trouble," he said.
"What kind of trouble?" I asked.

"You were found drunk on duty during my watch last night."

I drove out to the base and found the Navy Ensign who caught Willie the night before and explained what happened. I realized I had made a big mistake and asked him to overlook it this time. Somehow both Willie and I were let off the hook.

Willie went on to earn his wings and became a Navy pilot. He was killed in a crash during a night flight out of Elizabeth City, NC, flying an AD Skyraider.

* * *

Hank Dewey and I were Marine Corps captains together and in the same Squadron. He was a great big guy and had to kind of squeeze into the small cockpit of the A4 Skyhawks. I don't know what happened to Hank. I read in the Taps section of a Marine magazine he died. I felt sorry for his wife and kids.

* * *

Ed Jackson was one of the best pilots I ever knew, a Squadron mate and one of my best friends. Ed was a quiet tall guy with fire in his eyes and a cocky smirk on his face and reminded me of James Dean. He liked Jack Daniels. I was a gin drinker and we had many great times at Happy Hour. We competed as fighter/attack pilots. Sometimes he won and sometimes I won. We both excelled as nuclear delivery pilots and later I won the 2nd Marine Air Wing Top Gun award for "over the shoulder nuclear delivery." I always wondered if I would have won the award, had he lived to compete against me. His A4 flamed out and he tried to save the plane by crash-landing it. He was too low to eject and he plowed into the pine trees to avoid a school.

His wife Fran sued Douglas Aircraft because of the poor ejection capability. That lawsuit forced the company to design a rocket seat that could be used on the runway which saved the lives of many A4 pilots, including mine. They settled the lawsuit by paying Fran $50,000.00.

I was so upset that I couldn't go to his funeral. Instead I locked myself in my den with a bottle of Jack Daniels for a couple of hours.

* * *

Bob Kay was a nice kid in his twenties and a Lieutenant, but he looked like about seventeen, He looked so young we called him Cadet Kay. He was flying under ground control radar instructions while making an instrument approach to NAS Whidbey Island, WA, on a dark but clear night. He flew into the ground about one hundred yards short of the runway.

Dave Tierney, another Squadron pilot and I went to Whidbey Island to investigate the accident. We found a big hole in the ground and unfortunately found pieces of Bob Kay and had to put them in a body bag. We believed the base radar was partly at fault and proved our theory by duplicating his flight in another aircraft. Out of ten approaches, their radar would have run me into the ground twice if I had not looked out of my cockpit and pulled up. NAS Whidbey Island got new and updated radar a few months later as a result of our investigation.

During the same year, I had a similar experience when I flew to NAS Brunswick, Maine. An A4 pilot from another Squadron crashed after take off and hit a rock on the edge of a river a few miles from the base. I went to investigate that accident too. Same deal with the body bag.

One night after a long cold day out in the wilderness, I ventured into town and went to the Brunswick Hotel for some hot real New England clam chowder. It was delicious and I told the waiter it was the best clam chowder I ever had. He laughed and told me it was canned Snow's Clam Chowder.

* * *

Ed Loney was one of the best friends I have ever had. We called him "Old bullet" because he didn't move quickly but he always got the job done. Extremely dependable, he usually showed up on Saturday mornings after a late Friday night Happy Hour at 7:55 AM for an 8:00 AM tee off time and parred the first hole.

We were Squadron mates and flew many missions together in Vietnam and in all kinds of

Neil Levin

weather, he in his A4 and me in mine. We managed to survive getting shot at and all kinds of emergencies. Neither of us wanted to die in Vietnam and we didn't. We used to say, "I would rather get shot by a jealous husband."

He did. After he retired from the Marine Corps, he and his family moved to Virginia Beach and he got his real estate license. Working late one night in the office helping a fellow agent with a property, her enraged husband burst into the office, drew a .45 calibre pistol and shot and killed Ed.

* * *

A new Lieutenant joined the Squadron while we were in Vietnam. I forgot his name but I remember that he was extremely nervous. I led him into his first combat flight in North Vietnam. We made bombing runs on a truck park. I noticed he pulled out of his dives at a dangerously low altitude and even yelled at him to pull out. I also covered that with him during the de-briefing after the flight in the ready room.

The next day, with a different flight leader, he didn't pull out of a bombing run and crashed into a mountain. I believe he was so frightened, he had target fixation.

* * *

George Ward didn't fly into Vietnam with us but joined us later, assigned as our executive

206

officer. He was a tall, gray-haired, good looking, quiet guy with a good sense of humor and was a devoted family man. He was pretty much a "by the book" kind of Marine. He was in the back seat of a TA4 aircraft, which had two seats and used for such missions as reconnaissance. He flew at a low altitude and took a rifle round in the head.

* * *

Jerry Ruttlege built like a football player was also a Squadron mate and a real fun guy to be around. He became a flight instructor in the Navy's advanced jet fighter training program. He crashed after take off in an F9F-8 Cougar jet.

* * *

Tom Mulvihill was my mentor and my Commanding Officer in Vietnam. He was probably one of the most colorful people I ever knew. He could fly with the best of us and drink with the worst of us and he had a favorite saying for anything that came up. He was what we in the Marine Corps called a leader of men. He survived Vietnam but died in his sleep of a heart attack. I am sure if he could, he would have a favorite saying for that.

* * *

William Francis Mullen and I had lunch in our officer's mess, on the beach at Chu Lai. I just returned from a mission in North Vietnam and sat a table with Moon Mullen. At the time, I didn't know his first name but if your last name is Mullen, you're usually given the handle "Moon" after the famous cartoon character of yesteryear. We discussed my mission and the one he was going to fly up North after lunch. He flew it, was shot down over North Vietnam and never returned.

* * *

I finished a napalm attack and pulled off the target. I heard the mayday call from a pilot from another squadron, VMA 211. Hit bad and bleeding, he tried to nurse his A4 back to Chu Lai. I tried to catch up to him and kept talking to him on the radio. I spotted him ahead of me when suddenly he nosed over into a dive and crashed about thirteen miles from our home base of Chu Lai. His name was 1st Lt. Thomas Eldridge.

* * *

Jim McGarvey was an LSO, which means Landing Signal Officer, in charge of all of our training to prepare us for aircraft carrier landings. He was one of the best in the Marine Corps and more than one carrier skipper wanted him aboard. When he said you were ready to land day and night on an aircraft carrier‾ you were.

AN ANGEL RODE MY WING

He flew an A6 aircraft with another squadron in North Vietnam on a night mission when he was shot down. He left a wife and a whole bunch of kids.

* * *

There were more and one thing they all had in common besides being fighter/attack pilots was, they all died too young.

I mourn these people, especially on Memorial Day, but then again, another quote from General Patton, "Rather we thank God that such men lived."

They were real people and they had names.

THE LOVE OF FLYING

Ever since I was a little boy and my Dad took me flying in a small Piper Cub, I loved flying. I love everything about it. I love the smell of airplanes and the excitement I feel around airports whether they are for General Aviation or large Commercial Aviation. I love to be in the air and feel more free and at peace with myself than I do on the ground. It doesn't matter if I am the pilot in command of an airplane or a passenger in a Boeing 737, I just love being in the sky.

I don't ride in airplanes, I wear them while I fly. Even if I am a passenger, I sense each movement the pilot makes and I know when the landing gear or flaps are extended or retracted. I listen to the engine sounds and can anticipate power increases or decreases by the attitude of the airplane above or below the horizon and the rate of descent being too high or too low. I can anticipate the exact moment of lift off on take off and the moment of flare just before touch down on landing.

AN ANGEL RODE MY WING

I was a passenger in a small turboprop aircraft once and we took-off and climbed out of Fayetteville, North Carolina in a dense fog. I noticed the pilot didn't reduce power after takeoff to climbing power. We topped out at about 3000 feet and the plane kept climbing with full power. Knowing this was an unusual procedure, I looked out of the window to see what was going on. I noticed right away the landing gear that hung from under the wing on this particular type of aircraft was still extended, which increased the drag during the climb-out and the reason for the extra power in order to maintain climbing speed. A few reasons for the pilot not being able to retract the landing gear, including but not limited to, leaving the steel pins in place to assure the landing gear is locked in the down and safe position while the aircraft is parked on the ground. Since these pins have red flags attached to them and I didn't see any, I knew it wasn't the case. It could have been hydraulic pressure problems but there are backup systems to raise and lower the landing gear. I sensed the pilot concentrated so much on the takeoff in a dense fog he forgot to retract the landing gear.

I motioned the flight attendant. "Will you please go remind the pilot to pick up the landing gear?" I asked. "I believe he forgot to do it."

"Oh, he wouldn't forget that."

"Why don't you just go and ask him?"

He knocked on the cockpit door and after he stuck his head in the door the landing gear came right up.

The flight attendant returned with a sheepish grin. I gave a nod of approval

"Thank you," I said.

* * *

I recently took a flight on an airliner to West Palm Beach from San Diego. The purpose of my trip was to help celebrate my mother's 90th birthday. Most of my family was there from different parts of the country. It was great seeing everybody and honoring my mother. Incidentally, my mother told me she felt okay with being 90 years old because nobody ever asked her age. She actually looks and feels much younger, but dreads it when people ask her how old her children are though because that kind of gives her age away.

Choosing to live on the West Coast means I seldom see my children or grandchildren so this trip was even more of a special treat for me and I thoroughly enjoyed the flight.

I am not the type of person to brag about his kids or grandkids. They are all very special to me, each in their own way but so are other people's kids and grandkids.

My granddaughter, Julia Ann, seven years old, was the perfect age to be a sweet loveable grandchild. Whenever I see her I think of an Angel, because she is so loveable and so beautiful with her flowing blonde hair and milky white skin and adorable smile that she is quick to use. When she sees me, she takes a flying leap right into my arms and I melt right there on the spot.

Her mother Donna, who of course is my daughter, told me she read some of the articles I wrote for this book to Julia Ann and Christopher, my grandson. Julia Ann told her mother she already knew all about my flying adventures such as me being shot down.

"Julia, how could you know about what happened to Pop Pop?" Donna asked.

"Mother, before I was born I was an Angel in Heaven and I used to look down and I could see my Pop Pop. I watched him flying. I watched him get shot down and I watched his men coming to get him. There were some bad men coming to get him too. I watched to make sure his men got to him before the bad men did."

When I heard this, I got teary eyed. Of course, the child probably listened to my stories and then again, maybe not. I like to think she was the Angel that protected me.

As I look back at the many times I have somehow managed to survive extreme danger and life threatening situations during my twenty-year military flying career, I must admit one thing.

I do believe an Angel Rode My Wing.

ABOUT THE AUTHOR

Raised in the East, Neil left the Philadelphia College of Pharmacy and Science during the Korean War to begin a twenty-year career in Marine Aviation, including two combat tours of duty in Vietnam.

Father of four and wanting to share his adventures, he started to write short stories in 1996 of which seven were published. He lives in Oceanside, California.